Excel 2007:
Basic

Student Manual

Summit Computer
Training & Services

Congratulations on completing your training in **Excel Basic 2007.** We
hope you have enjoyed training with Summit CTS. **Remember, you
have one year of unlimited free phone and e-mail support which
expires May 16, 2010.** Simply contact Summit CTS at the e-mail address
number listed below. Also, you may re-take the class one time in the
next year at no charge.*
Call Summit CTS for class schedules and more details.
*Certain terms and conditions apply.

Support@SummitCTS.com ◆ 260.755.6409

Excel 2007: Basic

Series Product Managers:	Charles G. Blum and Adam A. Wilcox
Writer:	Steve English
Developmental Editor:	Micky Markert
Copyeditor:	Catherine Oliver
Keytester:	Cliff Coryea
Series Designer:	Adam A. Wilcox
Scholz	

Trademarks

ILT Series is a trademark of Axzo Press.

Microsoft is a trademark or registered trademark of Microsoft Corporation in the United States and/or other countries.

Some of the product names and company names used in this book have been used for identification purposes only and may be trademarks or registered trademarks of their respective manufacturers and sellers.

Disclaimers

We reserve the right to revise this publication and make changes from time to time in its content without notice.

Axzo Press is independent from Microsoft Corporation, and not affiliated with Microsoft in any manner. While this publication may be used in assisting individuals to prepare for a Microsoft Business Certification exam, Microsoft, its dedicated program administrator, and Axzo Press do not warrant that use of this publication will ensure passing a Microsoft Business Certification exam.

Student Manual
ISBN-10: 1-4239-1810-X
ISBN-13: 978-1-4239-1810-3

Student Manual with data CD and CBT
ISBN-10: 1-4239-1812-6
ISBN-13: 978-1-4239-1812-7

Printed in the United States of America

1 2 3 4 5 6 7 8 9 10 GLOB 10 09 08

What is the Microsoft Business Certification Program?

The Microsoft Business Certification Program enables candidates to show that they have something exceptional to offer—proven expertise in Microsoft Office programs. The two certification tracks allow candidates to choose how they want to exhibit their skills, either through validating skills within a specific Microsoft product or taking their knowledge to the next level and combining Microsoft programs to show that they can apply multiple skill sets to complete more complex office tasks. Recognized by businesses and schools around the world, over 3 million certifications have been obtained in over 100 different countries. The Microsoft Business Certification Program is the only Microsoft-approved certification program of its kind.

What is the Microsoft Certified Application Specialist Certification?

The Microsoft Certified Application Specialist Certification exams focus on validating specific skill sets within each of the Microsoft® Office system programs. The candidate can choose which exam(s) they want to take according to which skills they want to validate. The available Application Specialist exams include:

- Using Microsoft® Windows Vista™
- Using Microsoft® Office Word 2007
- Using Microsoft® Office Excel® 2007
- Using Microsoft® Office PowerPoint® 2007
- Using Microsoft® Office Access 2007
- Using Microsoft® Office Outlook® 2007

What is the Microsoft Certified Application Professional Certification?

The Microsoft Certified Application Professional Certification exams focus on a candidate's ability to use the 2007 Microsoft® Office system to accomplish industry-agnostic functions, for example Budget Analysis and Forecasting, or Content Management and Collaboration. The available Application Professional exams currently include:

- Organizational Support
- Creating and Managing Presentations
- Content Management and Collaboration
- Budget Analysis and Forecasting

What do the Microsoft Business Certification Vendor of Approved Courseware logos represent?

Microsoft
CERTIFIED
*Application
Specialist*

Approved Courseware

Microsoft
CERTIFIED
*Application
Professional*

Approved Courseware

The logos validate that the courseware has been approved by the Microsoft® Business Certification Vendor program and that these courses cover objectives that will be included in the relevant exam. It also means that after utilizing this courseware, you may be prepared to pass the exams required to become a Microsoft Certified Application Specialist or Microsoft Certified Application Professional.

For more information

To learn more about the Microsoft Certified Application Specialist or Professional exams[1], visit www.microsoft.com/learning/msbc.

To learn about other Microsoft Certified Application Specialist approved courseware from Axzo Press, visit www.axzopress.com.

[1]The availability of Microsoft Certified Application exams varies by Microsoft Office program, program version, and language. Visit www.microsoft.com/learning for exam availability.

Microsoft, Windows Vista, Excel, PowerPoint, and Outlook are either registered trademarks or trademarks of Microsoft Corporation in the United States and/or other countries. The Microsoft Certified Application Specialist and Microsoft Certified Application Professional logos are used under license from Microsoft Corporation.

Contents

Introduction

After reading this introduction, you will know how to:

A Use ILT Series training manuals in general.

B Use prerequisites, a target student description, course objectives, and a skills inventory to properly set your expectations for the course.

C Re-key this course after class.

Topic A: About the manual

ILT Series philosophy

ILT Series computer training manuals facilitate your learning by providing structured interaction with the software itself. While we provide text to explain difficult concepts, the hands-on activities are the focus of our courses. By paying close attention as your instructor leads you through these activities, you will learn the skills and concepts effectively.

We believe strongly in the instructor-led class. During class, focus on your instructor. Our manuals are designed and written to facilitate your interaction with your instructor, and not to call attention to manuals themselves.

We believe in the basic approach of setting expectations, delivering instruction, and providing summary and review afterwards. For this reason, lessons begin with objectives and end with summaries. We also provide overall course objectives and a course summary to provide both an introduction to and closure on the entire course.

Manual components

The manuals contain these major components:

- Table of contents
- Introduction
- Units
- Course summary
- Quick reference
- Glossary
- Index

Each element is described below.

Table of contents

The table of contents acts as a learning roadmap.

Introduction

The introduction contains information about our training philosophy and our manual components, features, and conventions. It contains target student, prerequisite, objective, and setup information for the specific course.

Units

Units are the largest structural component of the course content. A unit begins with a title page that lists objectives for each major subdivision, or topic, within the unit. Within each topic, conceptual and explanatory information alternates with hands-on activities. Units conclude with a summary comprising one paragraph for each topic, and an independent practice activity that gives you an opportunity to practice the skills you've learned.

The conceptual information takes the form of text paragraphs, exhibits, lists, and tables. The activities are structured in two columns, one telling you what to do, the other providing explanations, descriptions, and graphics.

Course summary

This section provides a text summary of the entire course. It is useful for providing closure at the end of the course. The course summary also indicates the next course in this series, if there is one, and lists additional resources you might find useful as you continue to learn about the software.

Quick reference

The quick reference is an at-a-glance job aid summarizing some of the more common features of the software.

Index

The index at the end of this manual makes it easy for you to find information about a particular software component, feature, or concept.

Manual conventions

We've tried to keep the number of elements and the types of formatting to a minimum in the manuals. This aids in clarity and makes the manuals more classically elegant looking. But there are some conventions and icons you should know about.

Item	Description
Italic text	In conceptual text, indicates a new term or feature.
Bold text	In unit summaries, indicates a key term or concept. In an independent practice activity, indicates an explicit item that you select, choose, or type.
`Code font`	Indicates code or syntax.
`Longer strings of ▶ code will look ▶ like this.`	In the hands-on activities, any code that's too long to fit on a single line is divided into segments by one or more continuation characters (▶). This code should be entered as a continuous string of text.
Select **bold item**	In the left column of hands-on activities, bold sans-serif text indicates an explicit item that you select, choose, or type.
Keycaps like ↵ ENTER	Indicate a key on the keyboard you must press.

Hands-on activities

The hands-on activities are the most important parts of our manuals. They are divided into two primary columns. The "Here's how" column gives short instructions to you about what to do. The "Here's why" column provides explanations, graphics, and clarifications. Here's a sample:

Do it!

A-1:   Creating a commission formula

Here's how	Here's why
1 Open Sales	This is an oversimplified sales compensation worksheet. It shows sales totals, commissions, and incentives for five sales reps.
2 Observe the contents of cell F4	F4 ▼ = =E4*C_Rate
	The commission rate formulas use the name "C_Rate" instead of a value for the commission rate.

For these activities, we have provided a collection of data files designed to help you learn each skill in a real-world business context. As you work through the activities, you will modify and update these files. Of course, you might make a mistake and therefore want to re-key the activity starting from scratch. To make it easy to start over, you will rename each data file at the end of the first activity in which the file is modified. Our convention for renaming files is to add the word "My" to the beginning of the file name. In the above activity, for example, a file called "Sales" is being used for the first time. At the end of this activity, you would save the file as "My sales," thus leaving the "Sales" file unchanged. If you make a mistake, you can start over using the original "Sales" file.

In some activities, however, it might not be practical to rename the data file. If you want to retry one of these activities, ask your instructor for a fresh copy of the original data file.

Topic B: Setting your expectations

Properly setting your expectations is essential to your success. This topic will help you do that by providing:

- Prerequisites for this course
- A description of the target student
- A list of the objectives for the course
- A skills assessment for the course

Course prerequisites

Before taking this course, you should be familiar with personal computers and the use of a keyboard and a mouse. Furthermore, this course assumes that you've completed the *Windows XP: Basic* course or have equivalent experience.

Target student

The target student for this course should be comfortable using a personal computer and Microsoft Windows XP. You should have little or no experience using Microsoft Excel or any other spreadsheet program. You will get the most out of this course if your goal is to become proficient in using Microsoft Excel to create simple worksheets and charts for internal reports and data tracking.

Microsoft Certified Application Specialist certification

This course is designed to help you pass the Microsoft Certified Application Specialist exam for Excel 2007. For comprehensive certification training, you should complete all of the following courses:

- *Excel 2007: Basic*
- *Excel 2007: Intermediate*
- *Excel 2007: Advanced*

Course objectives

These overall course objectives will give you an idea about what to expect from the course. It is also possible that they will help you see that this course is not the right one for you. If you think you either lack the prerequisite knowledge or already know most of the subject matter to be covered, you should let your instructor know that you think you are misplaced in the class.

Note: In addition to the general objectives listed below, specific Microsoft Certified Application Specialist exam objectives are listed at the beginning of each topic (where applicable). To download a complete mapping of exam objectives to ILT Series content, go to: www.virtualrom.com/658ACD612

After completing this course, you will know how to:

- Start Microsoft Excel; identify the main components of the Excel window and an Excel workbook; use the Help feature; and navigate worksheets.

- Enter and edit text, values, formulas; insert pictures in a worksheet; use AutoFill; and save and update a workbook.

- Move and copy data; insert and delete ranges; and work with relative and absolute references when creating and copying formulas.

- Use the SUM function, the AutoSum button, and the AVERAGE, MIN, MAX, COUNT, and COUNTA functions to perform calculations in a worksheet.

- Format text, numbers, rows, and columns in a worksheet; use conditional formatting; copy formats; and use table formats.

- Preview and control Page Setup options for a worksheet; check spelling; find and replace data; print a worksheet; and set and clear a print area.

- Create, format, modify, and print charts based on worksheet data.

- Manage large worksheets and multiple worksheets.

Skills inventory

Use the following form to gauge your skill level entering the class. For each skill listed, rate your familiarity from 1 to 5, with five being the most familiar. *This is not a test.* Rather, it is intended to provide you with an idea of where you're starting from at the beginning of class. If you're wholly unfamiliar with all the skills, you might not be ready for the class. If you think you already understand all of the skills, you might need to move on to the next course in the series. In either case, you should let your instructor know as soon as possible.

Skill	1	2	3	4	5
Starting Microsoft Excel					
Identifying rows, columns, cell references, and the active cell					
Accessing and using Help					
Opening, saving, and closing workbooks					
Entering and editing text, values, formulas					
Inserting, moving, and resizing pictures					
Using AutoFill					
Moving and copying data					
Inserting and deleting ranges					
Using relative and absolute references in formulas					
Using the SUM, AVERAGE, MIN, MAX, COUNT, and COUNTA functions					
Formatting text					
Formatting numbers					
Applying cell borders					
Changing column width and row height					
Checking spelling in worksheets					
Finding the synonyms of a word					
Previewing and printing worksheets					
Controlling Page Setup, including headers and footers					
Creating charts based on worksheet data					
Changing chart types					
Formatting chart elements					

Skill	**1**	**2**	**3**	**4**	**5**
Printing charts					
Freezing panes, splitting worksheets, and hiding and unhiding data					
Setting print titles and page breaks					
Navigating and printing multiple worksheets					
Renaming and color-coding worksheet tabs					
Inserting, copying, moving, and deleting worksheets					

Topic C: Re-keying the course

If you have the proper hardware and software, you can re-key this course after class. This section explains what you'll need in order to do so, and how to do it.

Hardware requirements

Your personal computer should have:

- A keyboard and a mouse
- Pentium 500 MHz processor (or higher)
- 256 MB RAM (or higher)
- 2 GB of available hard drive space
- CD-ROM drive
- SVGA at 1024 × 768, or higher resolution monitor

Software requirements

You will need the following software:

- Microsoft Windows XP, Service Pack (SP) 2 or later; Windows Vista; or Windows Server 2003
- Microsoft Office 2007

Network requirements

The following network components and connectivity are also required for this course:

- Internet access, for the following purposes:
  - Updating the Windows operating system and Microsoft Office 2007 at update.microsoft.com
  - Downloading the Student Data files (if necessary)
  - Opening Help files at Microsoft Office Online. (If online Help is not available, you will not be able to complete Activity C-1 in the unit titled "Getting started.")

Setup instructions to re-key the course

Before you re-key the course, you will need to perform the following steps.

1 From the Control Panel, open the Display Properties dialog box and apply the following settings:
   - Theme — Windows XP
   - Screen resolution — 1024 by 768 pixels
   - Color quality — High (24 bit) or higher

   If you choose not to apply these display settings, your screens might not match the screen shots in this manual.

2   Verify that Internet Explorer is the default Web browser.

    a   Click Start and choose All Programs, Internet Explorer.

    b   Choose Tools, Internet Options.

    c   Check "Internet Explorer should check to see whether it is the default browser."

    d   Click OK to close the Internet Options dialog box.

    e   Close and re-open Internet Explorer.

    f   If a prompt appears, asking you to make Internet Explorer your default browser, click Yes.

    g   Close Internet Explorer.

3   Connect to the Internet. An e-mail account is not required.

5   Open Internet Explorer and navigate to update.microsoft.com. Update the operating system with the latest critical updates and service packs.

6   Download the Student Data files for the course. (If you do not have an Internet connection, you can ask your instructor for a copy of the data files on a disk.)

    a   Connect to www.courseilt.com/ilt_downloads.cfm.

    b   Click the link for Microsoft Excel 2007 to display a page of course listings, and then click the link for Excel 2007: Basic.

    c   Click the link for downloading the Student Data files, and follow the instructions that appear on your screen.

7   Create a folder named Student Data at the root of the hard drive. For a standard hard drive setup, this will be C:\Student Data.

8   Copy the data files to the Student Data folder.

9   To ensure that you won't get a security warning when you open files in Excel, designate the Student Data folder as a Trusted Location:

    a   Click the Office Button and choose Excel Options to open the Excel Options dialog box.

    b   On the Trust Center page, click Trust Center Settings. The Trust Center dialog box opens.

    c   Navigate to the Trusted Locations page.

    d   Click Add new location. The Microsoft Office 2007 Trusted Location dialog box opens.

    e   Click Browse and navigate to the Student Data folder.

    f   Click OK to close the Browse dialog box.

    g   Check "Subfolders of this location are also trusted."

    h   Click OK to close the Microsoft Office 2007 Trusted Location dialog box.

    i   Click OK to close the Trust Center dialog box.

    j   Click OK to close the Excel Options dialog box.

    k   Close Excel.

CertBlaster exam preparation software

If you plan to take the Microsoft Certified Application Specialist exam for Excel 2007, we encourage you to use the CertBlaster pre- and post-assessment software that comes with this course. To download and install your free software:

1 Go to www.courseilt.com/certblaster.

2 Click the link for Excel 2007.

3 Save the .EXE file to a folder on your hard drive. (Note: If you skip this step, the CertBlaster software will not install correctly.)

4 Click Start and choose Run.

5 Click Browse and then navigate to the folder that contains the .EXE file.

6 Select the .EXE file and click Open.

7 Click OK and follow the on-screen instructions. When prompted for the password, enter **c_602**.

Unit 1

Getting started

Unit time: 30 minutes

Complete this unit, and you'll know how to:

A Identify spreadsheet components.

B Identify the main components of the Excel window.

C Use the Help feature.

D Open and navigate workbooks.

Topic A: Spreadsheet terminology

Explanation   Excel is an electronic spreadsheet program that is part of the Microsoft Office suite. You use Excel to organize, calculate, and analyze data. The tasks you can perform range from preparing a simple invoice to creating elaborate 3-D charts to managing an accounting ledger for a company.

In Excel, you work with *worksheets*, which consist of rows and columns that intersect to form *cells*. Cells contain various kinds of data that you can format, sort, and analyze. You can also create charts based on the data contained in cells. An Excel file is called a *workbook*, which by default contains three worksheets.

Components of a spreadsheet

All spreadsheets, whether on ledger paper or in an electronic spreadsheet program, have certain components in common. Exhibit 1-1 shows some of these common elements.

Exhibit 1-1: Spreadsheet components

The following table describes spreadsheet components and terms.

Item	Description
Row	A horizontal group of cells in a worksheet. There are more than a million rows in a worksheet. Each row is identified by a row number.
Column	A vertical group of cells in a worksheet. Each column is identified by one or more letters. The 26th column is column Z. The 27th is AA. When all of the double letters are used up, through ZZ, triple letters begin with AAA. There are more than 16,000 columns in a worksheet, ending with column XFD.
Cell	The intersection of a row and a column. A cell is identified by its column letter followed by its row number. For example, in Exhibit 1-1, the label "Name" is in cell A1.
Label	Text that identifies information in the spreadsheet. For example, in Exhibit 1-1, the labels in row 1 define the type of data in each column.
Value	The raw data in a spreadsheet. For example, in Exhibit 1-1, $5,767 in cell E3 is the value of third-quarter sales by Alan Monder.

Do it!

A-1: Discussing spreadsheet terminology

Here's how	Here's why
1 Observe the spreadsheet shown in Exhibit 1-1	This is a list of employees and their bonus sales for four calendar quarters.
2 Observe the column letters	They appear across the top of the spreadsheet and identify the columns below them.
3 Observe the row numbers	They appear on the left side of the spreadsheet and identify the rows to the right of them.
4 Observe the cells	Each cell occurs at the intersection of a column and a row. Cell A1, for example, contains the text "Name."
Observe cell D4	Cell D4 is the active cell, where the insertion point is located. The column letter and row number are highlighted, and a box appears around the cell.
5 Observe the labels	Column and row labels identify information in the spreadsheet. The labels in cells A1 through G1 identify information such as name, employee number, and calendar quarter.
6 Observe the values	Values are the raw data in a spreadsheet.
7 Observe the totals	Totals are calculations based on other values in the spreadsheet. For example, cell C5 contains the total sales for the first quarter, and cell G2 contains the total sales for employee Kendra James. You use formulas to perform calculations.

Topic B: Exploring the Excel window

Explanation

The Excel window has several features that help you use the program. However, the first thing you need to know is how to start Excel.

Starting Excel 2007

To start Excel, click Start and choose All Programs, Microsoft Office, Microsoft Office Excel 2007. A new workbook called "Book1" appears in the Excel window. You can also start Excel by double-clicking an Excel file.

Components of the Excel window

The components of the Excel window interact with the program or display information about what you are working on. Exhibit 1-2 shows the workbook window, and Exhibit 1-3 shows a close-up of some of these components, which are described in the following table.

Item	Description
Title bar	Displays the name of the workbook. The default name of the first workbook you open is "Book1."
Quick Access toolbar	Displays commands for saving the current workbook, undoing the last action, and repeating the last action. You can customize the Quick Access toolbar by adding buttons for frequently used commands. The Quick Access toolbar can be moved below the Ribbon.
Ribbon	Is the main location for menus and tools. Each Ribbon tab contains groups of commands or functions. Within each group are buttons and commands.
Gallery	Provides icons or other graphics to show the results of commands or options.
Formula bar	Displays the contents—such as values, formulas, or labels—of the active cell. You use this bar to edit the contents of the active cell.
Worksheet	Displays rows and columns of cells. Cells can contain values, text, and formulas.
Status bar	Displays the workbook's current status. The status bar might also display information about a selected command or an operation in progress. In addition, the status bar displays tools you can use to switch the view of the current document, switch to other documents, and zoom in and out on the current document.

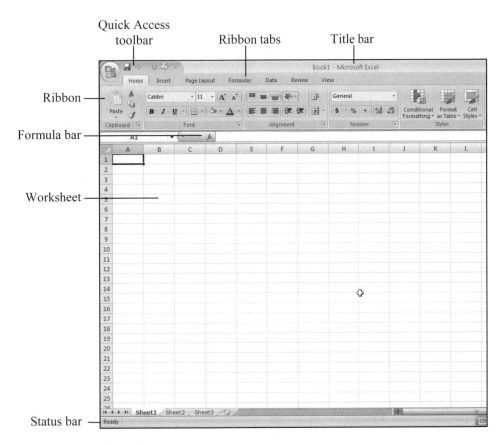

Exhibit 1-2: Excel window components

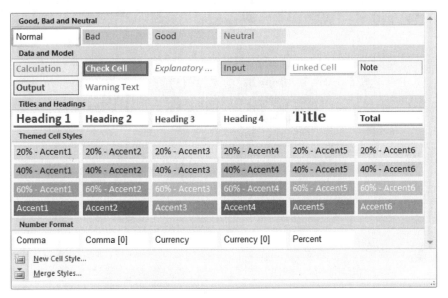

Exhibit 1-3: The Cell Styles gallery

Interacting with Excel

You interact with Excel by typing and by using the mouse to choose commands, make selections, and click buttons and options.

Using the Ribbon and galleries

The *Ribbon* is the main location for menus and tools. When you choose a Ribbon *tab*, the Ribbon displays *groups* that contain sets of related tools. (See Exhibit 1-4.) Some tools are buttons you click to perform a task immediately. Some tools expand to display simple lists or menus, and some tools display galleries.

A *gallery* is a collection of commands or options that are represented graphically to show the results of those commands or options. For example, the Cells Styles gallery, shown in Exhibit 1-3, shows the various built-in styles you can apply to cells.

Using Live Preview

The *Live Preview* feature enables you to see the results of formatting options before you apply them. For lists or galleries that use Live Preview, when you move the pointer over the options, each option's effect is shown on whatever is selected in the worksheet. For example, if you select text and display the Font list, pointing to a font in the list causes the selected text to appear in that font temporarily, as shown in Exhibit 1-4.

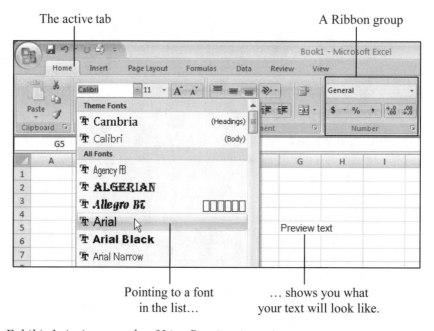

Exhibit 1-4: An example of Live Preview in action

Using tools

When you point to a tool, a description called an Enhanced ScreenTip appears. As illustrated in Exhibit 1-5, the Enhanced ScreenTip provides less description than Help, but more than an ordinary ScreenTip.

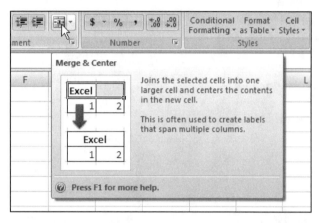

Exhibit 1-5: The Enhanced ScreenTip for the Merge & Center button

Do it!

B-1: Examining Excel window components

Here's how	Here's why
1 Click **Start** and choose **All Programs**, **Microsoft Office**, **Microsoft Office Excel 2007**	To start Microsoft Excel.
Maximize the window	If necessary.
2 Observe the title bar	Book1 - Microsoft Excel
	It shows the name of the current workbook, "Book1," and the name of the program, "Microsoft Excel."
3 Observe the Ribbon tabs	By default, Home is active.
Observe the Home tab	The Home tab contains Ribbon groups for Clipboard, Font, Alignment, Number, Styles, Cells, and Editing.
4 Click the **Insert** tab	To activate it. Groups associated with the Insert command are displayed.
In the Illustrations group, click **Shapes**	To display the Shapes gallery. Selecting one of these will copy this shape to the active cell.
Activate the Home tab	(Click the Home tab.) To display the Home tab's groups again.
5 In the Clipboard group, point to the clipboard icon above **Paste**, as shown	Paste (Ctrl+V) — Paste the contents of the Clipboard.
	An Enhanced ScreenTip appears for the Paste button. The Enhanced ScreenTip includes the button name, its keyboard shortcut, and a description.

6 Observe the formula bar	(The formula bar is below the Ribbon, as shown in Exhibit 1-2.) It displays the data in the active cell. The active cell, A1, currently has no data in it.
7 Observe the status bar	(The status bar is near the bottom of the Excel window, as shown in Exhibit 1-2.) It provides information about selected commands and the current status of the workbook. The status bar also contains tools for switching the view of the current document, switching to other documents, and zooming in and out on the current document.

Topic C: Getting help

Explanation

Excel provides a comprehensive Help system to support you as you work. You can use the Help window while offline (to open Help files on your hard disk) or while connected to the Internet (to display Help and other resources from the Microsoft Web site).

The Microsoft Excel Help window

Excel contains a help database from which it retrieves information. The *help database* is a collection of topics. It contains answers to frequently asked questions about Microsoft Excel 2007 and its interactions with other Office programs. You can use the Help window to search for specific content by using keywords or by selecting from a list of topics in the table of contents.

To open the Help window, click the Microsoft Excel Help button in the screen's top-right corner. An Excel Help topic is shown in Exhibit 1-6.

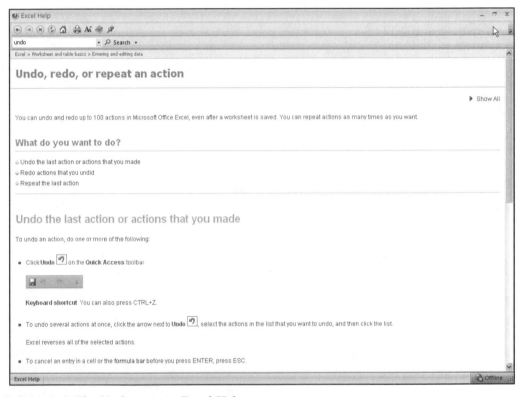

Exhibit 1-6: The Undo topic in Excel Help

Help on the Web

If your computer is connected to the Internet, you can access Help on the Web. You can get Help for Excel, retrieve worksheet templates, or take advantage of Excel training that is available from Microsoft.

To access Microsoft Help on the Web, choose Excel Help from the Search list, as shown in Exhibit 1-7. You'll be connected to Help on the Microsoft Office site, where you can find several links for getting help and troubleshooting problems.

Exhibit 1-7: Microsoft Excel Help provides Help, templates, and training

Do it!

C-1: Using Help

Here's how	Here's why
1 Click 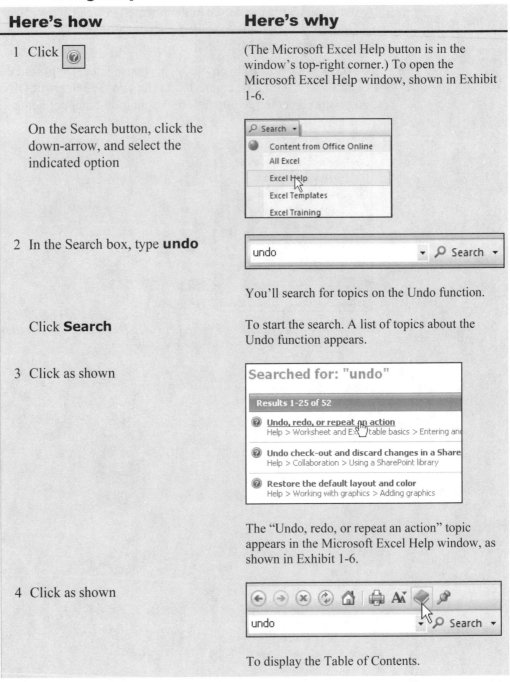	(The Microsoft Excel Help button is in the window's top-right corner.) To open the Microsoft Excel Help window, shown in Exhibit 1-6.
On the Search button, click the down-arrow, and select the indicated option	
2 In the Search box, type **undo**	
	You'll search for topics on the Undo function.
Click **Search**	To start the search. A list of topics about the Undo function appears.
3 Click as shown	
	The "Undo, redo, or repeat an action" topic appears in the Microsoft Excel Help window, as shown in Exhibit 1-6.
4 Click as shown	
	To display the Table of Contents.

5 In the Table of Contents, click
Worksheet and Excel table basics

(If necessary.) The icon beside the topic changes from a closed book to an open book, and a list of subtopics appears below the topic.

Click as shown

> 📖 Entering and editing data
> 　❷ Enter data manually in worksheet cell
> 　❷ Insert a symbol, fraction, or special c
> 　❷ Fill data automatically in worksheet ce
> 　❷ Insert or delete cells, rows, and colur
> 　❷ Edit cell contents
> 　❷ Turn automatic completion of cell entr
> 　❷ Wrap text in a cell

To display the Help topic on editing cell contents.

6 Observe the screen

(Maximize the window, if necessary.) The right-hand panel displays the requested information.

7 Click [x]

To close the Microsoft Excel Help window.

Topic D: Navigating workbooks

This topic covers the following Microsoft Certified Application Specialist exam objective for Excel 2007.

#	Objective
1.4.1	**Change views within a single window**
	• Change zoom level

Opening workbooks

Explanation

To begin working in an Excel workbook, you first need to open it. You can use the Office Button to open workbooks.

To open a workbook:

1 Click the Office Button and choose Open to display the Open dialog box, shown in Exhibit 1-8.

2 Use the Look in list to specify the folder containing the workbook you want to use.

3 Select the workbook and click Open (or double-click the workbook name).

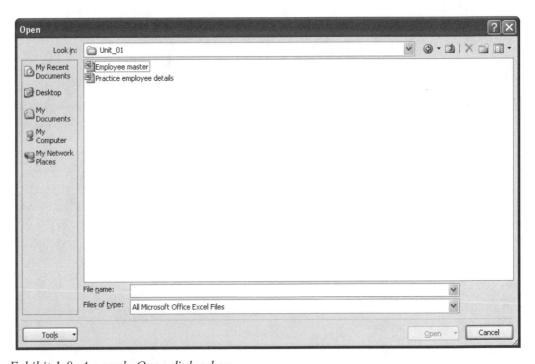

Exhibit 1-8: A sample Open dialog box

Moving around in worksheets

At any given time, one cell in the worksheet is the active cell. The active cell is where the data you enter will appear. The address of the active cell appears in the Name box, which is to the left of the formula bar.

There are several techniques for moving around in a worksheet. Some navigation techniques make a different cell active, while others move only your view of the worksheet, without activating a different cell.

The following table summarizes various worksheet navigation techniques:

Technique	Result
Click a cell	Makes the cell active.
Press arrow key	Selects an adjacent cell, making it active.
Press Tab	Select the cell one column to the right.
Press Shift+Tab	Selects the cell one column to the left.
Press Ctrl+Home	Selects cell A1.
Press Ctrl+End	Selects the cell at the intersection of the last row and last column of data in a worksheet.
Click the scroll arrow	Moves the view of the worksheet one row or column. This technique does not change the active cell.
Click in the scrollbar	Moves the view of the worksheet one screen up, down, left, or right, depending on which side of the scroll box you click (and in which scrollbar). This technique does not change the active cell.
Drag the scroll box	Moves the view of the worksheet quickly without changing the active cell.
Press Ctrl+G (or choose Edit, Go To)	Opens a dialog box where you can enter the address for a cell you want to move to.
Drag the slider on the zoom bar	Zooms in or out on the current document. The zoom bar is located on the status bar, near the bottom-right corner of the window.

Do it!

D-1: Navigating a worksheet

Here's how	Here's why
1 Click	The Office Button is located in the upper-left corner of the window.
Choose **Open**	To display the Open dialog box.
2 Navigate to the current unit folder and select **Employee master**	(Exhibit 1-8 shows the Look in list in the Open dialog box.) The current unit folder is in the Student Data folder.
Click **Open**	To open the workbook.
3 Observe the active cell	It is the cell with the dark outline—in this case, A1.
Observe the Name box	(The Name box is on the far left side of the formula bar.) It shows the address of the active cell, A1.
4 Press ↓	(The down arrow key.) To move down one row. The active cell is now A2.
Press ↑	To move up one row. Now the active cell is A1.

5 Click the down scroll arrow, as shown

This moves your view of the window down a row, but does not change the active cell.

Drag the vertical scroll box down

(The vertical scroll box is located in the right-hand scrollbar.) To quickly change your view of the worksheet without changing the active cell.

Return the scroll box to its original position

6 On the Home tab, in the Editing group, choose **Find & Select**, **Go To...**

To open the Go To dialog box. You'll use this dialog box to move to a distant cell in the worksheet.

In the Reference box, type **A43**

Click **OK**

To move to cell A43, the last data row in the worksheet.

Press ⌈CTRL⌉ + ⌈HOME⌉

To return to cell A1.

7 Press ⌈CTRL⌉ + ⌈END⌉

To move to the intersection of the last row and last column of data in a worksheet. This is useful in moving to the end of a list of data so that you can enter more data.

Return to cell A1

Press Ctrl+Home.

8 Drag the slider for the zoom bar to the left	(Located on the status bar in the bottom-right corner of the window.) To see all of the data in this worksheet without scrolling.
Continue dragging until rows 1–43 in the worksheet become visible	
Click the percentage number on the zoom bar	
	To open the Zoom dialog box.
Select **100%** and click **OK**	To return to 100% magnification.
9 Experiment with various navigation techniques	Use the table preceding this activity.
10 Press (CTRL) + (HOME)	To make A1 the active cell again.
11 Click [icon] and choose **Close**	To close the workbook. A dialog box appears, asking if you want to save the workbook.
Click **No**	(If necessary.) To close the workbook without saving any changes.
12 Click [icon]	
Click **Exit Excel**	To close Excel.

Unit summary: Getting started

Topic A   In this topic, you learned that **spreadsheets** can help you organize, calculate, and analyze data. You also learned about the **common features** of all spreadsheets, including rows, columns, cells, values, labels, and formulas.

Topic B   In this topic, you learned how to start Excel. You learned about the components of the Excel window, and you learned how to interact with Excel by using the **Ribbon**, which is divided into **tabs** and **groups**. You learned that **galleries** provides icons or other graphics to show the results of commands or options, and that some galleries and lists provide a **Live Preview**. You also learned how to display Enhanced ScreenTips for Ribbon buttons.

Topic C   In this topic, you learned about the **Help** system. You learned how to use the Help window. You also learned about getting help on the Web.

Topic D   In this topic, you learned how to open and **navigate** a workbook. You learned how to identify the **active cell** and observe its address in the **Name box**. You also learned how to navigate through a worksheet by using the keyboard and the mouse.

Independent practice activity

In this activity, you'll open an Excel file, navigate within that file, use Help, and close the file.

1 Start Excel.

2 Open the file Practice employee details (located in the current unit folder).

3 Activate cell B30.

4 Use Help to get information on opening a file.

5 Use the Find & Select group to navigate to F23. Return to A1.

6 Close Practice employee details. If prompted to save changes, click No.

7 Close Excel.

Review questions

1 What is the difference between a worksheet and a workbook?

2 What is a Ribbon group?

3 What is an active cell?

4 What key combination would you use to return to cell A1?

5 What menu choice or key combination would you use to move to a specific cell that is at the far end of the current worksheet?

Unit 2

Entering and editing data

Unit time: 45 minutes

Complete this unit, and you'll know how to:

A Create an Excel workbook, and enter and edit text and values in a worksheet.

B Enter and edit formulas in a worksheet.

C Insert, move, and resize pictures in a worksheet.

D Save and update a workbook, and use the Compatibility Checker.

Topic A: Entering and editing text and values

Explanation

After you create a workbook, you can begin entering data in cells. Cell entries can include many types of data, including text and values. When you type, data is entered in the active cell.

Text and values

Text entered in cells can be any length required, and it can be formatted just as in a word processing program; size, font, and style can all be changed. By default, text in a cell is left-aligned, as shown in Exhibit 2-1.

Values can include numbers, formulas, and functions. (Formulas and functions are explained in detail later.) Excel recognizes cell data as a value when it's a number or when it begins with +, -, =, @, #, or $. By default, a value in a cell is right-aligned.

	A	B	C	D	E	F
1	**Outlander Spices**					
2	**Bonus sales for the northern region**					
3						
4						
5						
6	Name	Emp #	Qtr1	Qtr2	Qtr3	Qtr4
7	Kendra James	16	$6,354	$4,846	$3,958	$8,284
8	Alan Monder	22	$7,546	$6,574	$5,767	$6,234
9	Audrey Kress	27	$7,635	$4,765	$5,256	$7,865
10	Julie George	29	$9,595	$5,859	$4,879	$3,432

Exhibit 2-1: A sample worksheet with text and values

Overflowing text and values

If a long text string doesn't fit in a cell, it will appear to go into the next cell if that cell is empty. The text isn't really in that next cell, though. If there is data in that next cell, the long string of text is truncated to fit the cell it's in.

If a long value doesn't fit in a cell, Excel displays a row of # characters. This indicates that the cell is too narrow to display the value, as shown in Exhibit 2-2.

The formula bar shows that D1, the active cell, is actually empty

The text in A1 apears to go into adjacent cells

That same text entered in A4 is truncated by the presence of text in B4

Values that are too long for a cell are replaced with a row of #s

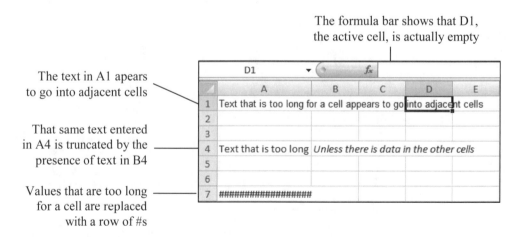

Exhibit 2-2: Text and values that are too long for their cells

The Num Lock key

The numeric keypad, on the right side of most computer keyboards, is controlled by a Num Lock key in the upper-left corner of the keypad. Press Num Lock once to switch the keypad from functioning as numeric keys to functioning as navigation keys. Press Num Lock again to return to numbers. When numbers are active, a Num Lock light typically lights on the keyboard, as shown in Exhibit 2-3.

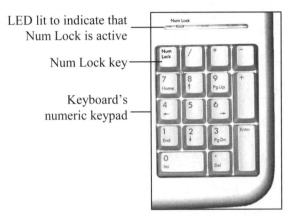

LED lit to indicate that Num Lock is active

Num Lock key

Keyboard's numeric keypad

Exhibit 2-3: The Num Lock key on a keyboard's numeric keypad

Do it!

A-1: Entering text and values

Here's how	Here's why
1 Start Excel	(Click Start and choose All Programs, Microsoft Office, Microsoft Office Excel 2007.) The title bar displays "Book1," which is the name of the default workbook.
Click [icon] and choose **Close**	To close the workbook. You'll create a new one.
2 Click [icon] and choose **New**	To open the New Workbook dialog box.
3 Double-click **Blank Workbook**	To create a new workbook. The name of the new workbook, "Book2," appears in the title bar.
4 Select B1	(Click it.) To make B1 the active cell. The cell address B1 appears in the Name box.

5 Type **Outlander Spices**	To specify a heading for the worksheet. The text (or any other data) overlaps other blank cells if it takes up more room than the cell size allows. However, Excel considers the data to be the content of only the cell where you entered it—in this case, B1.
Press (↵ ENTER)	To complete the entry and move to B2. By default, text entries are left-aligned.
6 Select A4	To make A4 active.
Type **Month**	To create text that labels this column.
Press (↵ ENTER)	To complete the entry and move to A5.
7 Type **January**	To create text that labels this row.
8 In B4, enter **Region1**	The active cell now is B5.
9 In B5, enter **21000**	

	A	B	C
1		Outlander Spices	
2			
3			
4	Month	Region1	
5	January	21000	
6			

(Name box: B6)

To enter the Region 1 sales for January. The workbook should look like the picture shown here.

Editing text and values

Explanation

If you make an error while entering data in a cell, you can correct it at any point. To make corrections, you can do any of the following:

- Double-click the cell, make the corrections, and press Enter.
- Click the formula bar, make the corrections (as shown in Exhibit 2-4), and press Enter.
- Select the cell and type the correct data.

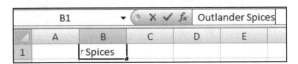

Exhibit 2-4: The formula bar showing B1 being modified

The Clear command

You can use the *Clear* command to remove a cell's contents, formats, comments, or all three. When a cell is cleared, its value is zero. To clear a cell:

1. Activate the Home tab (if necessary).
2. In the Editing group, click the Clear button, shown in Exhibit 2-5.
3. Choose one of the following four options:
   - Clear All removes the cell contents, as well as any formats and comments.
   - Clear Formats removes the cell's formats but not the contents.
   - Clear Contents removes the cell's text or value but not the formats.
   - Clear Comments removes any comments but not the contents or formats.

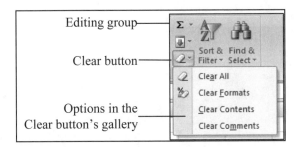

Exhibit 2-5: The options in the Clear button's drop-down menu

It's easy to delete the contents of a cell without using the Clear command. Just select the cell and press Delete (located just above the arrow keys on most keyboards). If multiple cells are selected, pressing Delete will clear the contents of all of them.

A-2:   Editing text

Here's how	Here's why
1 In A2, enter **Extra sales projections**	To add text to the worksheet.
2 Select A2	You'll modify the contents of this cell.
Select **Extra** in the formula bar, as shown	⬤ X ✓ *fx* **Extra** sales projections
	To edit the text.
Type **Bonus**	To change the text to "Bonus sales projections."
3 Press (END)	To move the insertion point to the end of the text, where you'll add more text.
Press (SPACEBAR)	To add a space before the new text.
Type **for the northern region**	To add this text.
Press (↵ ENTER)	The text now reads "Bonus sales projections for the northern region."
4 Enter **Final Version** in A3	Type "Final Version" and press Enter.
5 Enter **Confidential** in C3	
6 Select A3	You'll remove the text from A3 and C3.
Press (CTRL) and select C3	

	A	B	C	D	E
1		Outlander Spices			
2	Bonus sales projections for the northern region				
3	Final Version		Confidential		

Holding the Ctrl key while you click the mouse causes both cells to be selected. The outline box surrounds the current cell. Any other cells that have been selected are shaded.

7 Press (← BACKSPACE)	

	A	B	C	D	E
1		Outlander Spices			
2	Bonus sales projections for the northern region				
3	Final Version				

Only the contents of the current cell are cleared. The text in the other selected cell remains.

Press (ESC)	To undo the Backspace action and restore the contents of C3.

8 Click 🖉 ▾   (The Clear button is in the Editing group.) To
                                    display the Clear menu.

   Choose **Clear All**   To clear both contents and formats from the
                                    selected cells.

AutoFill

When you need to enter a list of numbers, dates, days of the week, or other sequential data, you can use the AutoFill feature to complete the list, as shown in Exhibit 2-6.

The *fill handle* is a small square in the lower-right corner of a selected cell or range. When you point to the fill handle, the pointer changes to a plus sign (+). The fill handle can autofill a range to complete a list or series.

To use AutoFill:

1   Select the cell containing the value that starts the list or series.
2   Point to the fill handle until the pointer changes to a + symbol.
3   Drag the fill handle over the adjacent cells that you want to fill.

For numbers or dates, you can select two cells with a desired range, and AutoFill will continue with the same increments. For example, you could use this technique to fill a range by 10s or to fill a range with dates a week apart.

	A	B	C	D	E
1		Outlander Spices			
2	Bonus sales projections for the northern region				
3	Final Version				
4	Month	Region1	Region2	Region3	Region4
5	January	21000			
6	February				
7	March				
8	April				
9	May				
10	June				
11	July				
12	August				
13	September				
14	October				
15	November				
16	December				
17					

Exhibit 2-6: Using AutoFill to insert a list of months

Do it!

A-3: Using AutoFill to fill a series

Here's how	Here's why
1 Select B4	It contains the text "Region1." You'll use AutoFill to add more headings.
2 Point to the fill handle, as shown	 The pointer takes the shape of a plus sign (+).
3 Press and hold the mouse button	
Drag the fill handle to the right to E4, as shown	 As you drag, a shaded outline appears around the range you're filling. As you drag past each cell, a screen tip displays what will be entered in each cell.
Release the mouse button	To finish autofilling the cells for the remaining regions.
4 Select A5	You'll autofill the remaining months in the year.
Autofill to cell A16	(Drag the fill handle to A16.) The cells are populated with the months of the year, as shown in Exhibit 2-6.
5 Click ⊞ and choose **Close**	To close the workbook. A message box appears, prompting you to save the workbook.
6 Click **No**	To close the workbook without saving it.

Topic B: Entering and editing formulas

Explanation

Formulas perform numeric calculations, such as adding, multiplying, and averaging. All formulas in Excel begin with the equal sign (=). A formula can refer to a value, a cell address, or another formula. *Functions* are predefined formulas that perform string operations or calculations, which can be simple or complex. Many formulas contain *operators*—characters that indicate the type of arithmetic operation the formula will perform.

The following table shows the types of arithmetic operators you can use:

Operator	Used for...	Example
+	Addition	=A7+A9
-	Subtraction	=A7-A9
*	Multiplication	=A7*A9
/	Division	=A7/A9
%	Percentages	=50%
^	Exponents	=5^3 means 5 raised to the third power (5^3), or 5*5*5

Entering formulas

To enter a formula, select the cell where you want the result to appear. Then type the formula and press Enter. For example, if there are numbers in A2 and A3, and you want to add them and show the result in A4, you select A4, type =A2+A3, and press Enter. The result appears in A4. If A4 is the active cell, the formula appears in the formula bar (as shown in Exhibit 2-7).

Formulas are based on the values contained in the cells in your worksheet. If you change the cells that a formula refers to, the result of the formula will change.

Exhibit 2-7: A sample formula, showing the result in the active cell and the formula in the formula bar

Do it!

B-1: Entering a formula by typing

Here's how	Here's why
1 Open Sales	Click the Office Button and choose Open. Navigate to the current unit folder, and double-click Sales in the Open dialog box.
2 Select G5	To activate the cell where you'll enter a formula.
Type **=**	To indicate that you're about to enter a formula rather than text or a value.
3 Type **C5+D5+E5+F5**	This formula adds the values of the quarterly bonus sales for Kendra James; these values are in cells C5 through F5.
Press ↵ ENTER	The result of the formula is $23,442.00.
4 Select G5	f_x =C5+D5+E5+F5
	The formula bar shows the formula, not the result.
5 Select F5	You'll change one of the cells in the formula.
Type **1000**	
Press ↵ ENTER	The result of the formula in G5 automatically changes to $16,158.00.

Using the mouse to enter cell references in formulas

Explanation

You can use the mouse to enter cell references for a formula. To do so:

1   Select the cell where you want to enter the formula.
2   Type = (to begin a formula).
3   Click the cell for which you want to enter a reference.
4   Type the operator you want.
5   Repeat Steps 3 and 4 until you've created the formula you want.
6   Press Enter.

Do it!

B-2:   Entering cell references with the mouse

Here's how	Here's why
1 Select G6	You'll enter a formula to calculate the total quarterly bonus sales for Pamela Carter.
Type **=**	To begin the formula.
2 Select C6	To enter this cell's address in the formula you're creating.
Type **+**	To continue to build the formula.
3 Select D6	To enter D6 in the formula.
4 Complete the formula as shown, using the mouse to enter the cells	f_x =C6+D6+E6+F6
Press (↵ ENTER)	To enter the formula. G6 now contains the total quarterly bonus sales for Pamela Carter. G9 contains $40,913.00, which is the total of the values in G5 and G6.
5 In G7, enter a formula to calculate the total bonus sales for Julie George	Use any method you like. When you are finished, G7 should contain $23,765.

Editing formulas

Explanation

Formulas can be edited to adapt to changes in the worksheet or to correct a mistake. Edit a formula as you would edit any other cell. Simply double-click the cell and enter the correct formula. You can also edit a formula by using the formula bar:

1. Select the cell containing the formula.
2. Edit the formula in the formula bar.
3. Press Enter.

Do it!

B-3: Editing a formula

Here's how	Here's why
1 Observe G9	The total displayed in this cell is incorrect.
2 Select G9	You'll edit the formula in this cell.
Observe the formula bar	The formula bar shows =G5+G6. This formula doesn't include the total for Julie George.
3 Place the insertion point at the end of the formula	X ✓ ƒ_x =G5+G6
4 Type**+G7**	To add the G7 cell value to the formula.
Press ⏎ ENTER	
5 Observe G9	G9 now shows the correct value, $64,678.00.

Topic C: Working with pictures

This topic covers the following Microsoft Certified Applications Specialist exam objective for Excel 2007.

#	Objective
4.4.1	**Insert and modify pictures from files**
	• Insert pictures
	• Modify pictures

Using pictures in worksheets

Explanation

You can insert pictures and other graphics files to illustrate and enhance worksheets and printed reports, as shown in Exhibit 2-8. Excel supports dozens of industry-standard picture file formats, including .bmp, .jpg, .eps, and .tif.

	A	B	C	D	E	F	G
1				Outlander Spices			
2			**Bonus sales in the northern region**				
3							
4	Name	Emp #	Qtr1	Qtr2	Qtr3	Qtr4	Total
5	Kendra James	16	$6,354.00	$4,846.00	$3,958.00	$8,284.00	$23,442.00
6	Pamela Carter	25	$8,484.00	$5,858.00	$5,858.00	$4,555.00	$24,755.00
7	Julie George	29	$9,595.00	$5,859.00	$4,879.00	$3,432.00	$23,765.00

Exhibit 2-8: A worksheet with a picture

Adding pictures

To place a picture in a worksheet:

1. Activate the Insert tab.
2. In the Illustrations group, click the Insert Picture From File button. The Insert Picture dialog box appears.
3. Navigate to the picture's location, select the file, and click Insert. The picture appears in the worksheet, and the Picture Tools tab is activated.
4. Use the tools on the Picture Tools tab to modify the picture as necessary.

Moving pictures

When you insert a picture into a worksheet, Excel places it in the approximate middle of your screen. You can move a picture so that it appears and prints in a specific place in a worksheet. To move a picture:

1 Point anywhere within the picture. The pointer changes to a four-headed arrow.

2 Drag the picture. As you drag, the picture remains stationary, but a shadow of it moves with the pointer, as shown in Exhibit 2-9.

3 Position the outline box where you want the picture to be.

4 Release the mouse button. The picture moves to the location of the outline box.

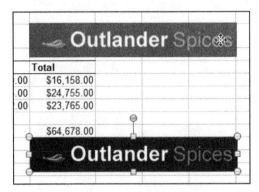

Exhibit 2-9: A gray outline box indicates where the picture will be moved to

Resizing pictures

There are several ways to resize a picture:

- Select the picture; this activates the Picture Tools tab. In the Size group, enter new values in the Height and Width boxes.

- In the Size group, click the Dialog Box Launcher button (in the lower-right corner of the group). The Size and Properties dialog box appears with the Size tab activated. Under Size and Rotate, or under Scale, resize the picture.

- Point to one of the sizing handles at the corners of the picture frame. The pointer changes to a double-headed arrow. Drag a sizing handle to resize the picture.

To resize a picture proportionally, click and hold Shift before dragging the sizing handles. This forces the picture's height and width to resize at the same rate.

Do it!

C-1: Inserting and modifying a picture

Here's how	Here's why
1 Activate the Insert tab	You'll insert a logo picture in this worksheet.
2 Click [Picture]	(The Insert Picture From File button is in the Illustrations group.) The Insert Picture dialog box appears.
Navigate to the current unit folder	
Select **logo**	From the current unit folder.
Click **Insert**	To insert the picture. The logo appears in the middle of the worksheet, and the Picture Tools tab is activated.
3 In the Size group, observe the picture dimensions	
	The picture is 0.49 inches tall and 3.02 inches wide.
4 Point to the handle in the lower-right corner of the picture, as shown	
	The pointer changes to a double-headed arrow.
Press and hold (SHIFT)	
Drag up and to the left slightly	To proportionally resize the picture.
5 Observe the picture dimensions	In the Size group.
Resize the picture proportionally until it is approximately the height of three rows	
	Press Shift and drag the picture handle in or out to get the desired size.

6	Point anywhere inside the picture	The pointer changes to a four-headed arrow.
	Drag up and to the left	A shadow of the picture moves with the pointer.
	Move the upper-left corner of the outline box to the upper-left corner of B1	Where the words "Outlander Spices" appear.
7	Click anywhere in the worksheet	To deselect the picture. The worksheet should resemble Exhibit 2-8.

Topic D: Saving and updating workbooks

This topic covers the following Microsoft Certified Applications Specialist exam objective for Excel 2007.

#	Objective
5.4.1	**Save workbooks for use in a previous version of Excel**
	• Using Compatibility Checker, determine which feature of a workbook is incompatible with a previous version
	• Save a specific feature to the Excel 97-2003 format

Saving workbooks

Explanation

Saving a workbook stores your data for future use. Every time you change anything in a worksheet, you'll need to save the worksheet (update it) if you want to keep your changes.

Saving a file for the first time

The first time you save a workbook, you need to assign a file name and location for the file. You must also choose a file format. Some typical file formats include:

Format	Extension	Description
Microsoft Excel Workbook	.xlsx	This is the default workbook format for Excel 2007.
XML Data	.xml	The XML format is useful for data that must be transferred between applications.
Text	.txt	Files saved in plain text format can be opened by any word processor or text editor.
Comma Separated Values	.csv	Data fields in a CSV file are delimited by commas.
Excel 97 - Excel 2003 Workbook	.xls	This is the workbook format that can be opened by earlier versions of Excel.
Web Page	.html	This format enables the workbook to be published as a Web page.

To save a workbook for the first time:

1   Click the Office Button and choose Save, or click the Save button on the Quick Access toolbar. The Save As dialog box opens (as shown in Exhibit 2-10) because this file does not yet have a file name.

2   From the Save in list, select the drive and folder where you want to save the workbook.

3   In the File name box, enter a name for the workbook.

4   From the Save as type list, select the file format in which you want to save the workbook.

5   Click Save.

Creating folders

If you don't want to save your workbook in an existing folder, use the Save As dialog box to create a new folder. Here's how:

1   From the Save in list, select the location where you want to create the folder.

2   In the Save As dialog box, click the Create New Folder button to open the New Folder dialog box.

3   In the Name box of the New Folder dialog box, type a name for the folder.

4   Click OK. The new folder appears in the Save in list.

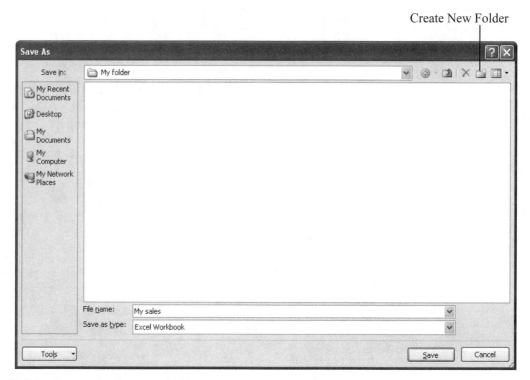

Exhibit 2-10: The Save As dialog box

Do it!

D-1: Saving a workbook

Here's how	Here's why
1 Open a new blank workbook	Click the Office Button and choose New, or press Ctrl+N.
2 Click 🖫	(The Save button is on the Quick Access toolbar, near the top-left corner of the workbook.) To save the workbook.
Observe the Save in box	The last folder you accessed is active and, unless changed, will be the location for your file. You can select various special folders from the left side of the dialog box.
In the File name box, enter **My saved file**	
Click **Save**	To save the file with the name and location you specified.
3 Observe the title bar	My saved file - Microsoft Excel
	The new file name is displayed.
Click ⊠	(The Close button is in the upper-right corner of the file window.) To close the file.
4 Click and choose **Save As**	To open the Save As dialog box. You'll save the Sales file with a different name and in a different location.
5 Click 📄	(The Create New Folder button is on the toolbar in the Save As dialog box.) To open the New Folder dialog box.
In the Name box, type **My folder**	To name the new folder.
Click **OK**	Save in: 📁 My folder
	The name of the folder you created appears in the Save in box.
6 In the File name box, type **My Sales**	This is the new name for the file.
Click **Save**	To save the file.
7 Observe the title bar	It displays the workbook's name.

Updating workbooks

Explanation   Each time you save a workbook, Microsoft Excel updates the workbook file with the latest changes. You should update your workbooks frequently so that changes aren't lost. To save changes in a workbook, click the Save button on the Quick Access toolbar or press Ctrl+S.

Do it!   ### D-2:   Changing and updating a workbook

Here's how	Here's why
1 In A10, enter **Annual target**	To add text to the worksheet.
2 Click [💾]	To update the workbook with the newly added text.
3 Open the Save As dialog box	(Click the Office Button and choose Save As.) You'll save a copy of the workbook with a different name.
4 In the File name box, type **My annual target**	To specify a different name for the workbook.
Click **Save**	To save the workbook.
5 Observe the title bar	The name of the current workbook, "Annual target," now appears in the title bar.
6 Close the workbook	Click the Office Button and choose Close.

Previous versions of Excel

Explanation

Workbooks created in Excel 2007 are not compatible with previous versions of Excel. You can, however, save a workbook created in Excel 2007 as an Excel 97-2003 workbook to enable people with earlier versions to open and use it.

To save a workbook in the Excel 97-2003 Workbook format, click the Office Button and choose Save As, Excel 97-2003 Workbook. The Save As dialog box opens, with Excel 97-2003 Workbook selected in the "Save as file type" box. Enter a name for the workbook, if necessary, and click Save. In the Save as type list, select Excel 97-2003 Workbook.

The Compatibility Checker

Not all features present in Excel 2007 workbooks can be saved in the 97-2003 workbook format. You can check which features are incompatible with earlier versions of Excel by running the Compatibility Checker, shown in Exhibit 2-11.

There are two way to use the Compatibility Checker to determine which Excel 2007 features are incompatible with earlier versions of Excel:

- Click the Office Button and choose Prepare, Run Compatibility Checker.
- Click the Office Button and choose Save As, Excel 97-2003 Workbook to open the Save As dialog box. Click Save. If the workbook has any features that cannot be saved in the file format for the earlier version of Excel, the Compatibility Checker will launch, notifying you of any problems.

If it's possible to correct the feature, the Compatibility Checker will display the Fix option. You can choose whether to fix the issue or leave it as is. If you leave the feature as is, however, it will not be displayed properly when the workbook is opened in the earlier version of Excel.

You can configure the Compatibility Checker to run automatically whenever you update the workbook. Just check "Check compatibility when saving this workbook" in the Compatibility Checker dialog box.

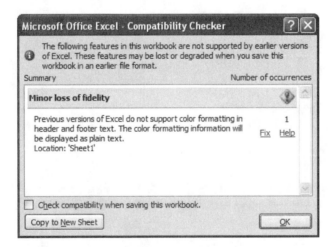

Exhibit 2-11: The Compatibility Checker

Do it!

D-3: Using the Compatibility Checker

Here's how	Here's why
1 Open 97 Sales	In the current unit folder. You'll save this workbook in the Excel 97-2003 Workbook format.
2 Observe the worksheet	The header contains the current date and the word "Confidential" formatted in blue.
3 Click ⊞	
Choose **Prepare**, **Run Compatibility Checker**	To open the Microsoft Office Excel - Compatibility Checker dialog box. A message appears, stating that color formatting in header and footer text is not supported in previous versions of Excel.
4 Click **Fix**	To change the header text to black and correct the incompatibility.
5 Click **OK**	To close the dialog box and apply the change. The text is reformatted.
Click ⊞	
Choose **Save As**, **Excel 97-2003 Workbook**	To open the Save As dialog box. Excel 97-2003 Workbook is selected in the Save as type list.
6 Edit the file name to read **My 97 Sales**	
Click **Save**	To save the file in the new format with a new name.
Close the workbook	

Unit summary: Entering and editing data

Topic A   In this topic, you created a workbook and learned how to enter and edit **text and values** in a worksheet. You learned that, by default, text is left-aligned and values are right-aligned. You also learned how to edit a cell by clicking the **formula bar** and by double-clicking a cell. Then, you learned how to **autofill** a series.

Topic B   In this topic, you learned how to use **formulas** to perform calculations on values in a worksheet. You learned how to enter formulas and how to use an **operator** to combine values. You also learned how to use the mouse to enter **cell references** and how to edit formulas.

Topic C   In this topic, you learned how to insert a picture into a worksheet. You also learned how to **resize** a picture proportionally and how to move a picture in the worksheet.

Topic D   In this topic, you learned how to **save** and **update** a workbook to prevent data loss. In addition, you learned how to save a file with a different name and in a different location. Finally, you learned how to save workbooks in an earlier version of Excel, and how to run the **Compatibility Checker** to find features that might not be compatible with earlier versions.

Independent practice activity

In this activity, you'll create a workbook, enter data, create formulas, and save the workbook in both 2007 and 97-2003 formats.

1 Create a new workbook.

2 Enter data beginning in row 4, as shown in Exhibit 2-12.

3 In column E, enter formulas to calculate the total costs for each item. (*Hint*: The multiplication operator is *.) Compare your results to Exhibit 2-13.

4 Insert the picture file Outlander into the worksheet.

5 Resize the picture and position it as shown in Exhibit 2-13. (*Hint*: Resize the picture proportionally until it is approximately 1.65 inches wide.)

6 Save the workbook as **My total costs** in the current unit folder.

7 Save the workbook as an Excel 97-2003 Workbook, with the name **My total costs 97**.

8 Close the workbook.

	A	B	C	D	E
1					
2					
3					
4	Code	Desc	Quantity	Cost/Item	Total cost
5					
6	10001	Garlic	16	2.5	
7	12001	Cayenne	7	4	
8	13003	Dill	5	6	
9					

Exhibit 2-12: The data to be entered in Step 2

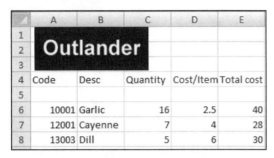

	A	B	C	D	E
1					
2	Outlander				
3					
4	Code	Desc	Quantity	Cost/Item	Total cost
5					
6	10001	Garlic	16	2.5	40
7	12001	Cayenne	7	4	28
8	13003	Dill	5	6	30

Exhibit 2-13: The formula results after Step 4

Review questions

1 Name two basic types of data that can be entered in a worksheet.

2 How can you clear a cell's text or value but not its formatting?

3 All formulas must begin with what symbol?

4 How do you resize a picture so that its dimensions remain proportional?

5 What is the default file-name extension for workbooks saved in Excel 2007?

Unit 3

Modifying a worksheet

Unit time: 45 minutes

Complete this unit, and you'll know how to:

A Move and copy data in a worksheet.

B Move and copy formulas in a worksheet.

C Use absolute references in formulas.

D Insert and delete ranges, rows, and columns in a worksheet.

Topic A: Moving and copying data

Explanation

You can move and copy data between cells, ranges, or worksheets or even from one workbook to another. Excel provides commands, buttons, and a drag-and-drop method for these purposes.

When you cut or copy data, Excel places that data on the Windows Clipboard. The *Clipboard* is a special memory area that can temporarily store one data item. When you specify a new location for the data, Excel copies the data from the Clipboard to that new location.

Moving data

You can move data by activating the Home tab and using the Cut and Paste buttons in the Clipboard group. Here's how:

1   Select the cell or data that you want to move.
2   Activate the Home tab, if necessary.
3   In the Clipboard group, click Cut (or press Crtl+X).
4   Select the cell that you want to move the data to. This cell is called the *destination cell*.
5   In the Clipboard group, click Paste (or press Ctrl+V).

You can use Cut (or Ctrl+X) only to move a cell's contents, not to delete the contents. Data that has been cut is not removed from the original cell until it is pasted into another cell.

Do it!

A-1: Moving data in a worksheet

Here's how	Here's why
1 Open Rearranging	(In the current unit folder.) You'll modify the data in this workbook.
Save the workbook in the current unit folder as **My rearranging**	
2 Select F12	You'll move the contents of this cell.
Activate the Home tab	If necessary.
Click ✂	(The Cut button is in the Clipboard group.) To cut the contents of F12.
Observe the marquee around F12	Spices ‌National Sales
	The moving, dashed boundary indicates that you have cut the cell data and it is now on the Clipboard.
3 Select F4	To specify the new location for the data.
Click 📋	(The Paste button is in the Clipboard group.) To paste the contents of F12 into F4. F12 is now empty.
4 Select D7	You'll move part of the text in this cell.
5 In the formula bar, select **and Marketing**, as shown	● ✗ ✓ *fx* Sales and Marketing
	You also need to select the space before "and."
Click ✂	To cut the selected text from D7.
Observe the formula bar	● *fx* Sales
	The selected text has been removed from D7.
6 Select D12	You'll paste the cut text at the end of the text in this cell.
Place the insertion point as shown	● ✗ ✓ *fx* Sales|
Click 📋	To paste the text into D12.
7 Click 💾	To update the workbook.

Copying data

Explanation
When you want to use the same data in several places, it's best to copy this data (for accuracy), rather than type it at each location. Data can be copied within a worksheet, between worksheets, between workbooks, and among other applications. You can copy all or part of a cell's contents.

Selecting multiple cells

You can select multiple cells simultaneously so that you can move, copy, paste, or format their contents. A *range* is a selection that includes multiple consecutive cells. To select a range, do either of the following:

- Point to the cell where you want the range to begin; then drag to the cell where you want the range to end.
- Click the cell where you want the range to begin. Press Shift and click the cell where you want the range to end.

When you select a range, a box appears around it and the range's cells are shaded.

A *range reference* is composed of the addresses of the first and last cells in the range, separated by a colon (:). For example, if you drag the mouse from A2 to H5, the reference is A2:H5.

To select cells that are *non-contiguous* (cells that are not adjacent to each other):

1   Select the first cell.
2   Press Ctrl and select the next cell.
3   Continue until all the cells you want are selected.

A box appears around the last cell selected. This is the active cell. All other selected cells are shaded.

Copying data

Data in one cell or range can be duplicated in another cell or a range. To copy data:

1   Select the data you want to copy.
2   Activate the Home tab.
3   In the Clipboard group, click Copy (or press Ctrl+C).
4   Select the destination cell for the data.
5   In the Clipboard group, click Paste (or press Ctrl+V).

When you paste the copied data, the Paste Options button appears beside the destination cell. When you click this button, a list of options appears.

Copying to the cell above

To copy and paste text or numbers in the cell immediately above the active cell, press Ctrl+' (Ctrl + apostrophe).

Do it!

A-2: Copying data in a worksheet

Here's how	Here's why
1 Select F4	You'll copy the text "National Sales" from here to F12.
Click	(The Copy button is in the Clipboard group.) To copy the contents of the selected cell. The marquee appears, indicating that you've copied the cell data to the Clipboard.
2 Select F12	This is the cell where you'll paste the copied text.
Click	To paste the copied text. "National sales" now appears in F12, while remaining in F4. Notice that the marquee is still visible; this indicates that you can paste another copy of the text in another location.
3 Copy A1 and paste in D1	
	(Select A1, click the Copy button, select D1, and click the Paste button.) The text is pasted in D1, but you want just the format pasted. The Paste Options button appears.
4 Click as shown	
	A list appears.
Observe the list	
	These options determine what is pasted in the destination cell.
Select **Formatting Only**	To paste only A1's text format in D1. The text "Employee info" disappears from D1.
5 In D1, enter **2006**	The text appears in Arial 14 Bold Italic—the same format as the text in A1.
6 Update the workbook	Click the Save button.

Using drag-and-drop

Drag-and-drop is a method of moving or copying data. *Dragging* is the act of pointing to a cell, pressing the mouse button, and moving the pointer without releasing the mouse button. *Dropping* is releasing the mouse button after the pointer reaches the destination cell.

To move a cell by using the drag-and-drop method:

1 Select the cell that contains the data you want to move.
2 Point to the border of the cell. The pointer changes to a four-headed arrow.
3 Drag the cell to where you want to move the data. As you drag, a cell outline will show where the data will go when you release the mouse button.
4 Release the button when the pointer reaches the destination cell.

To copy a cell's contents to another cell:

1 Select the cell that contains the data you want to copy.
2 Point to the border of the cell. The shape of the pointer changes.
3 Press and hold Ctrl. The pointer will now include a plus sign (+).
4 Drag to the destination cell.
5 When the pointer reaches the destination cell, release the mouse and then release Ctrl.

Do it!

A-3: Moving and copying data by using drag-and-drop

Here's how	Here's why
1 Select D17	You'll move the contents of this cell to D19.
2 Point to the edge of the cell, as shown	

The pointer changes to a four-headed arrow.

Press and hold the mouse button

While holding down the mouse button, drag to D19

The boundary of D19 appears shaded. Also, a ScreenTip tells you the address of the cell where the data will appear when you release the button.

Release the mouse button — To drop the data in D19. All the data from D17 has been moved here, and D17 is now empty.

3 Point to the edge of D19 — The pointer changes to a four-headed arrow.

Press and hold CTRL

The pointer displays a plus sign.

While holding CTRL, drag to D17

Release the mouse button and CTRL — To drop the copied data. D17 now contains the contents of D19, and D19 retains its contents.

4 Update the workbook

The Office Clipboard

Microsoft Office applications contain a special Clipboard, called the *Office Clipboard*. The Office Clipboard can hold any type of data that the Windows Clipboard can hold. Unlike the Windows Clipboard, which can hold only a single data item, the Office Clipboard can hold multiple items. Data items placed on the Office Clipboard are available to all open Microsoft Office applications.

To copy an item to the Office Clipboard, select the item and click the Copy button in the Clipboard group. When the items are on the Clipboard, you can then paste them one at a time or all at once.

The Collect and Paste feature

You can use the Collect and Paste feature to copy several items from any combination of Microsoft Office applications to a single location. For example, you might need to include content from a Microsoft Word document, a Web page, and a Microsoft PowerPoint presentation in a single worksheet. To do this, collect all the items in the Office Clipboard. You do this by switching to each of these sources and copying the items you need. Then, you can switch to the worksheet and paste the items from the Office Clipboard.

The Clipboard task pane

You can copy up to 24 items to the Office Clipboard. The Clipboard task pane displays all the items you've copied to the Office Clipboard in the current work session. The last item copied to the Office Clipboard is also copied to the Windows Clipboard. Even when you close the Clipboard task pane, its contents are not cleared. However, the Office Clipboard becomes inactive and the Windows Clipboard is used to copy and paste items.

You can view the Clipboard task pane by clicking the arrow button in the bottom-right corner of the Clipboard group or by pressing Ctrl+C twice.

The following table shows the buttons in the Clipboard task pane:

Button	What it does
Paste All	Pastes multiple items simultaneously.
Clear All	Clears the Clipboard.
Options ▼	Contains options that control how the Office Clipboard is displayed.

Do it!   **A-4: Copying data by using the Clipboard**

Here's how	Here's why
1 Click the arrow in the bottom-right corner of the Clipboard group, as shown	
	To display the Clipboard task pane.
2 If necessary, click **Clear All**	(The Clear All button is in the Clipboard task pane.) To clear the Clipboard.
3 Select A3:G3	(Drag from A3 to G3.) These cells contain the column headings. You'll copy the contents of these cells to the Clipboard.
Press CTRL + C	(Or click the Copy button in the Clipboard group.) To copy the contents of the range you selected to the Clipboard.
Observe the Clipboard pane	The items you just copied appear.
4 Copy the contents of A5:G9 to the Clipboard	These rows contain information about Bill MacArthur's team. Both copied items are now listed in the Clipboard task pane.
5 Click ⬛ and choose **New**	To open the New Workbook dialog box.
Double-click **Blank Workbook**	To create a workbook. You'll paste the items you copied to the Office Clipboard in this workbook.
In the Clipboard pane, click **Paste All**	

	A	B	C	D	E	F	G	H
1	Name		Emp #	Division	Region	Departme	Manager	
2	Shannon L		2 23-2328	Acquisitior	Home	Acquisitior	Bill MacArthur	
3	Melinda M		3 17-3312	Administra	Home	Administra	Bill MacArthur	
4	James Ove		4 42-5487	Sales and	Home	Sales and	Bill MacArthur	
5	Roger Will		5 36-8162	Support	Home	Support	Bill MacArthur	
6	Annie Phili		6 191-0128	Executive	Home	Executive	Bill MacArthur	

	The data you copied to the Clipboard appears in the new workbook.
6 Save the workbook as **My team**	In the current unit folder.
7 Close the Clipboard pane	Click the X in the upper-right corner of the task pane.
8 Update and close both workbooks	

Topic B: Moving and copying formulas

This topic covers the following Microsoft Certified Application Specialist exam objectives for Excel 2007.

#	Objective
1.1.2	Copy a series using AutoFill
3.1.1	Create formulas that use absolute and relative cell references
	• Create a formula that, when copied to an adjacent cell, updates its cell references to reflect its new location

Formulas in Excel

Explanation

A formula can contain references, values, operators, or functions. The formula in a cell determines the value to be displayed.

Formulas are moved in the same way as any other data. When the same formula is needed in several locations, copy it to those locations instead of retyping it in each cell.

Moving formulas

If you move a formula from one location to another, the calculation that was performed at the first location will be performed at the new location. Any references you used in the formula will remain the same. You can use shortcut menus to perform actions, such as moving data, more easily.

Using shortcut menus

For most of the elements of the screen, you can use the right mouse button to display a shortcut menu. A *shortcut menu* provides a short list of commands related to the object or screen element you right-clicked. For example, when you point to a selected cell and click the right mouse button, you'll see a shortcut menu containing the Cut and Copy commands.

Cutting and pasting vs. drag-and-drop

Cutting and pasting is usually most effective when the destination cell is not visible on the screen. If you have to scroll vertically or horizontally to locate the destination cell, use Cut and Paste to move a formula. For short moves across the current view, however, it's often easier to simply drag the formula to its destination cell and drop it there.

Do it!

B-1: Moving a formula

Here's how	Here's why
1 Open Formulas	In the current unit folder.
Save the workbook as **My formulas**	
2 In H5, enter **=C5+D5+E5+F5**	You'll move this formula to column G.
3 Select H5	To prepare to move the formula.
Right-click H5	To display a shortcut menu.
From the shortcut menu, choose **Cut**	A marquee appears around the cell.
4 Right-click H6	To display a shortcut menu for that cell.
Choose **Paste**	(From the shortcut menu.) The formula is moved to H6. You realize that's not the right place for this formula. Because it provides the total of C5:F5, it should be placed in the Total column at G5.
5 Select H6	If necessary.
Point to the cell border	
	The pointer changes to a four-headed arrow.
Drag to G5	To move the formula to its correct location.
6 Update the workbook	

Copying formulas

Explanation

You can copy and paste formulas to reuse them. Formulas are copied in the same way as any other data. Any references in the formula are adjusted to reflect the new location of the copied formula.

Relative cell references

A *reference* identifies a cell or a range of cells in a worksheet. The reference contains a set of coordinates that specify a cell's position. For example, when you refer to a cell as B2, it means that the position of that specific cell is where column B intersects row 2.

By default, Excel uses relative cell references in formulas. *Relative cell references* mean that when Excel checks the references in a formula you write, it sees those references in relation to the location of the formula.

Excel adjusts relative cell references when you copy a formula to a new location. For example, if you refer to cell C1 in a formula contained in D1, and you copy the formula to D2, the reference in the formula changes to C2 automatically.

Exhibit 3-1 shows how you write a formula.

	A3	▼			f_x	=A1+A2
	A	B	C	D		
1	10	20				
2	20	30				
3	30					
4						

Exhibit 3-1: A formula using a relative reference

When you copy a formula that uses relative references, Excel looks at the physical locations of those references. What the formula actually says is "add the value in the cell two rows up to the value in the cell one row up." When you copy the formula to B3, Excel still sees the formula in the same way. The difference is that the cell two rows up is B1, and the cell one row up is B2. The resulting formula is =B1+B2, as shown in Exhibit 3-2.

	B3	▼			f_x	=B1+B2
	A	B	C	D	E	
1	10	20				
2	20	30				
3	30	50				
4						

Exhibit 3-2: The copied formula

Do it!

B-2: Copying a formula

Here's how	Here's why
1 Select G5	If necessary.
Observe the formula bar	*fx* =C5+D5+E5+F5
	You'll copy this formula to G6. The references are all in row 5. These are relative references, and Excel will adjust them when you copy the formula to a new location.
2 Copy the formula	Use any method you like.
3 Select G6	
Paste the formula	
Observe the formula bar	*fx* =C6+D6+E6+F6
	The references are now all in row 6. Excel considers relative cell references in relation to their locations. The original formula added the values in the four cells to the left of it in the current row. This formula does the same.
4 Update the workbook	

Using the fill handle

Explanation

You can use the AutoFill feature, via the fill handle (shown in Exhibit 3-3), to copy a formula to adjacent cells. Here's how:

1 Select the cell containing the formula you want to copy.
2 Point to the fill handle until the pointer changes to a + symbol.
3 Drag the fill handle over the adjacent cells to which you want to copy the formula.

Exhibit 3-3: The fill handle

Do it!

B-3: Using AutoFill to copy a formula

Here's how	Here's why
1 Select G6	(If necessary.) It contains the formula =C6+D6+E6+F6.
2 Point to the fill handle, as shown	The pointer takes the shape of a plus sign (+). You can use the fill handle to copy this formula to adjacent cells.
3 Drag the fill handle to G7, as shown	As you drag, a shaded outline appears around the range you'll be filling with the copied data. An Auto Fill Options button appears.
Click as shown	To display the shortcut menu for Auto Fill Options. Copy Cells is selected by default.
Click the Auto Fill Options button again	To close the shortcut menu.
4 Select G7	Excel has adjusted the relative cell references so that the formula is now =C7+D7+E7+F7.
5 Update the workbook	

Topic C: Absolute and relative references

This topic covers the following Microsoft Certified Application Specialist exam objective for Excel 2007.

#	Objective
3.1.1	**Create formulas that use absolute and relative cell references**
	• Create a formula that maintains its reference point when copied to a new location
	• Create a formula with mixed relative and absolute references

Working with cell references

Explanation

Relative references are the default in Excel, and they make it simple for you to copy most formulas to several places. Sometimes, however, you won't want Excel to adjust references when you copy a formula. Instead, you'll want to copy the formula but have it keep its original references. To address this situation, Excel uses absolute references and mixed references.

Limitations of relative references

If a formula refers to a specific cell that should not change when you copy the formula, the copied formula will produce unexpected results when you paste it.

Using Undo

If you make a mistake in Excel, it is easy to reverse. Simply click the Undo button on the Quick Access toolbar, or press Ctrl+Z.

Do it!

C-1: Observing the limitations of relative references

Here's how	Here's why
1 Observe H2	It contains the sales reps' commission rate for bonus sales. You'll create formulas in column H to calculate actual commissions based on this rate.
2 In H5, enter **=G5*H2**	To calculate Kendra James's commission on bonus sales.
3 Select H5	You'll copy this formula to H6 and H7.
Drag the fill handle to H7	 To copy the formula down through the column.
4 Select H6	It displays $0.00. The formula multiplies Pamela Carter's total in G6 by H3, which has no value. This occurs because Excel adjusted this reference relative to the location of the new formula, resulting in an incorrect formula.
5 Select H7	It displays an error value. In this case, the references have been adjusted such that the formula multiplies the sales total by the text "Comm" in H4. An error indicator appears in the top-left corner of the cell.
6 Click 	To undo your last action, which was filling the formula down the column.
7 Update the workbook	

Absolute references

Explanation

When you don't want a reference to change when you copy it, you can use an *absolute reference*. To make a reference absolute, place a dollar sign in front of both the column letter and the row number of the reference. For example, to create an absolute reference to cell A1, you would enter A1 in a formula. When you copy an absolute reference to another location, Excel does not adjust the reference.

Mixed references

You can also create *mixed references* by placing a dollar sign in front of only the column letter or the row number. When you copy the formula, the relative part of the reference will adjust relative to the new location, and the absolute part will not. You can cycle through the reference possibilities by pressing F4 when you're entering a reference.

Do it!

C-2: Using absolute references

Here's how	Here's why
1 Select H5	(If necessary.) You'll adjust the reference to the commission rate to make it absolute.
2 Place the insertion point in the formula bar as shown	`× ✓ fx  =G5*H2`
Press F4	`× ✓ fx  =G5*$H$2`
	To change the cell reference to H2, making it an absolute reference.
Press ↵ ENTER	To enter the formula.
3 Select H5	
Copy the formula to H6 and H7	Use the fill handle.
4 Select H6	`fx  =G6*$H$2`
	H6 now displays the correct value. In the formula, the first reference was adjusted relative to the formula's location. However, the absolute reference, H2, remained unchanged.
5 Select H7 and observe the formula	This formula is also correct.
6 Update the workbook	

Topic D: Inserting and deleting ranges, rows, and columns

This topic covers the following Microsoft Certified Application Specialist exam objective for Excel 2007.

#	Objective
2.2.1	**Insert and delete cells, rows, and columns** • Insert a column or row above, below, to the left, or right of an existing column or row • Insert multiple rows or columns simultaneously

Working with rows, columns, and ranges

Explanation

A row, column, or range of cells can be inserted in or deleted from a workbook.

Inserting ranges

To insert a range of cells in a worksheet:

1 Select the range where you want to insert the cells. To select a range, point to the first cell you want to select, and drag to the last cell. Do not use the fill handle while dragging.

2 In the Cells group, on the Home tab, click Insert. You can also choose Insert from the shortcut menu for the selected range. Excel will display a dialog box with options for shifting the remaining cells.

3 Specify whether you want to shift cells or insert an entire row or column.

4 Click OK.

Do it!

D-1: Inserting a range

Here's how	Here's why
1 Select the range A6:H6	You'll insert a range of cells to store data for a new sales representative.
2 On the Home tab, in the Cells group, click as shown	
	To display the Insert menu.
From the menu, choose **Insert Cells...**	To open the Insert dialog box.
Observe the dialog box	
	You must specify which way to shift the selected cells. "Shift cells down" is selected by default.
Click **OK**	To insert the range and shift the cells down.
3 In row 6, enter the following data	

| 6 | Alan Monder | 22 | $7,500.00 | $6,550.00 | $5,700.00 | $6,200.00 |

4 Select the range G5:H5	You'll fill these formulas down to complete Alan Monder's data.
Drag the fill handle down to H6	

Total	Comm
$23,442.00	937.68
$24,755.00	990.20

To copy the total and commission formulas to Alan Monder's row.

5 Update the workbook

Inserting rows and columns

Explanation

To insert a row or column:

1 Select the row or column where you want to insert a new row or column. You can use the column and row heading buttons to select entire columns and rows.

2 Right-click the selected area to display a shortcut menu.

3 From the shortcut menu, choose Insert. You can also click the Insert button's down-arrow (in the Cells group) and choose Insert Sheet Rows or Insert Sheet Columns.

When you insert a row or column, you don't have to specify where to shift cells. The new row will be inserted above the selected row, and a new column will be inserted to the left of the selected column. If you want to insert multiple rows or columns simultaneously, select the number of rows or columns that equal the number of rows or columns you want to insert.

Do it!

D-2: Inserting rows

Here's how	Here's why
1 Select rows 5 through 8, as shown	
	You'll insert four rows simultaneously.
On the Home tab, in the Cells group, click the down arrow next to **Insert**	To display the Insert menu.
Choose **Insert Sheet Rows**	To insert four rows above the selected rows.
Click ↶	To undo the action.
2 Select row 8	Click the row heading for row 8.
3 Right-click the selection	To display a shortcut menu.
Choose **Insert**	To insert a row above the selected row. When you insert an entire row or column, you don't need to specify how to shift the remaining cells.
4 In row 8, enter the following data	

8	Audrey Cress	27	$7,500.00	$4,500.00	$5,200.00	$7,500.00

5 Copy the formulas from G7:H7 to G8:H8	To complete the new representative's data.
6 Update the workbook	

Deleting ranges

Explanation

If you don't need a range, you can delete it. To delete a range:

1 Select the range you want to delete.
2 In the Cells group, click Delete. You can also choose Delete from the shortcut menu.
3 Specify where to shift the adjacent cells.
4 Click OK.

If you are deleting an entire row or column, you don't need to specify where to shift cells.

Do it!

D-3: Deleting a range

Here's how	Here's why
1 Select A7:H7	A7:H7 contains the data for Pamela Carter.
2 Display the shortcut menu	Right-click the selection.
Choose **Delete...**	To open the Delete dialog box. "Shift cells up" is selected by default.
Click **OK**	To delete the selected range and shift the remaining cells up.
3 Undo the deletion	You'll perform the last action again, this time deleting the entire row.
4 Select row 7	Click the row-heading button.
From the shortcut menu, choose **Delete**	To delete the selected row. When you delete an entire row or column, you don't have to specify where to shift the remaining cells.
5 Update and close the workbook	

Unit summary: Modifying a worksheet

Topic A   In this topic, you learned how to move and copy data in a worksheet. You learned that you can do this by using the **Cut**, **Copy**, and **Paste** buttons in the Clipboard group. You also learned how to move and copy data by using the **drag-and-drop** method and the **Windows Clipboard**. You learned that you can use the **Office Clipboard** to copy multiple items simultaneously.

Topic B   In this topic, you learned that you move or copy formulas in the same way in which you move or copy any other data. You learned how to use **shortcut menus** to display common commands for a selection or screen element. You saw that because of **relative references**, Excel can adjust references in a copied formula relative to its new location. You also learned how to use the **fill handle** to copy data to adjacent cells.

Topic C   In this topic, you learned that for some formulas, relative references will not produce the desired results when you copy those formulas. You learned how to use **absolute references**, which are not adjusted when you copy a formula.

Topic D   In this topic, you learned how to insert and delete **ranges**. You learned that when you insert or delete a range, you must specify where to shift remaining cells. You also learned that you don't need to specify where to shift cells when you insert or delete an entire row or column.

Independent practice activity

In this activity you will insert a row and copy and delete data. You'll create a formula and copy it, using both relative and absolute references.

1 Open Practice southern sales and save it as **My practice southern sales**.

2 Insert a row above row 10.

3 Copy the data for 2006 sales to the inserted row. (*Hint*: Copy A15:E15.)

4 Delete the row containing the data for sales in the year 2001.

5 In cell F5, enter a formula to calculate the total sales for 2002.

6 Copy the yearly total formula to F6:F9.

7 In F10, enter a formula that will calculate the total sales for the five-year period. Use absolute references so that you'll be able to copy the formula without changing the references later.

8 Copy the formula in F10 to A19.

9 Change the value in B5 to 11000.

10 Observe the change in values in A19 and C19.

11 Compare your work with Exhibit 3-4.

12 Update and close the workbook.

	A	B	C	D	E	F	G
1		**Outlander Spices**					
2	**Yearly bonus sales for the northern region (all figures in $)**						
3							
4	Year	Qtr1	Qtr2	Qtr3	Qtr4	Total	
5	2002	11000	15478	18756	17563	62797	
6	2003	17895	19872	19653	19845	77265	
7	2004	22156	14235	15698	21036	73125	
8	2005	20789	12458	13698	18654	65599	
9	2006	9109	14825	16682	19295	59911	
10			Total of last five years			338697	
11							
12	**Sales for 2006**						
13	Year	Qtr1	Qtr2	Qtr3	Qtr4		
14	2006	9109	14825	16682	19295		
15							
16	**Profit earned in last five years**						
17							
18	Total of last five years	% Profit	Profit amount				
19	338697	20	67739.4				

Exhibit 3-4: The worksheet after Step 10 in the independent practice activity

Review questions

1 What is a range?

2 What is meant by the term "relative cell reference?"

3 Describe one limitation of a relative reference.

4 How do you designate a reference as an absolute reference?

5 List the steps you would use to delete a range.

Unit 4

Using functions

Unit time: 40 minutes

Complete this unit, and you'll know how to:

A Use the SUM function to calculate the sum of values.

B Use the AutoSum button to enter SUM functions.

C Use the AVERAGE, MIN, MAX, COUNT, and COUNTA functions to find average, minimum, and maximum values and the count of cells in a range.

Topic A: Entering functions

This topic covers the following Microsoft Certified Application Specialist exam objective for Excel 2007.

#	Objective
3.2.1	Use SUM, COUNT, COUNTA, AVERAGE, MIN, MAX
	• Sum

Benefits of using functions

Explanation

Performing calculations on each value in a range of cells can be complicated and time-consuming. For example, if you have a range consisting of 20 cells, a formula that adds each of these values will be very long. Excel functions simplify complex tasks. Also, if you insert cells within the range used in a function, the function automatically adjusts to include the new cells.

The structure of functions

A *function* is a predefined formula that performs a specific calculation or other action on a number or a text string. You specify the values on which the function performs the calculations.

Functions have the following structure, or syntax:

```
=FUNCTIONNAME(ARGUMENT1,ARGUMENT2,…)
```

Like formulas, functions begin with an equal sign. Following that is the name of the function and then a set of parentheses enclosing the input values for the function.

Arguments are the input values of a function. Arguments can be numbers, text, cell addresses, ranges, or other functions.

The SUM function

One of the most important functions available is *SUM*, which calculates the total of all the values listed in its arguments. It has the following structure:

```
=SUM(number1,number2,…)
```

For example, the function =SUM(2, 3) calculates the sum of 2 and 3, returning the value 5. Consider the data in Exhibit 4-1 and the functions in the table that follows.

	A
1	10
2	20
3	30
4	40

Exhibit 4-1: Sample data

Function	Result
=SUM(A1, A2)	30
=SUM(A1, A4)	50
=SUM(A2,100)	120

Entering range references

To enter a contiguous range of cells in a formula or function, type the first cell in the range, followed by a colon (:) and the last cell in the range. For example, in Exhibit 4-1, the sum of cells A1, A2, A3, and A4 is written as:

```
=SUM(A1:A4)
```

The Trace Error button

When there might be an error in a cell, Excel's error-checking feature warns you by displaying a green triangle, called the *error indicator*, in the top-left corner of the cell. When you select this cell, the Trace Error button appears; you can click it to display a list of actions you can perform on the formula. You can use this list to resolve the error or ignore it, or you can use one of the error-checking options available.

Syntax errors

A *syntax error* is one in which a formula or function is entered in the wrong form or is missing some required punctuation. When a function is entered incorrectly, Excel attempts to diagnose the error. If it appears to be a syntax error, Excel will suggest a solution. For example, if a function to sum cells A1 through A4 is written as

```
=SUM(A1;A4)
```

with a semicolon (;) instead of a colon (:), an error message appears, as shown in Exhibit 4-2.

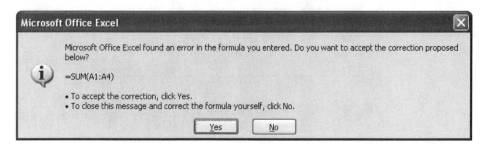

Exhibit 4-2: An Excel dialog box suggesting a solution for a simple syntax error

Do it!

A-1: Entering a SUM function

Here's how	Here's why
1 Open Functions	In the current unit folder.
2 Save the workbook as **My functions**	
3 Select G5	You'll enter a SUM function here to calculate Kendra James's sales total for the year.
4 Type **=**	All formulas, including functions, begin with the equal sign (=).
Type **SUM(**	To enter the name of the function and an opening parenthesis. A function argument ScreenTip appears as you type.
Type **C5:F5**	To enter a range reference as an argument for the function. The function will calculate the sum of the values in C5, D5, E5, and F5.
Type **)**	

f_x =SUM(C5:F5)

The closing parenthesis completes the function.

5 Press ↵ ENTER	To enter the function, returning the value 23442.
6 Select G5	An error indicator appears in the upper-left corner of the cell, and the Trace Error button appears beside the cell.
7 Point to the Trace Error button	

	23442
623	26121
786	
343	

The formula in this cell refers to a range that has additional numbers adjacent to it.

A long ScreenTip appears, describing the possible error in the cell formula.

8	Click the Trace Error button	To display a list of options.
	Observe the list	

◇ ▾ ┃   23442┃
Formula Omits Adjacent Cells
<u>U</u>pdate Formula to Include Cells
<u>H</u>elp on this error
<u>I</u>gnore Error
Edit in <u>F</u>ormula Bar
Error Checking <u>O</u>ptions...

The error Formula Omits Adjacent Cells is highlighted in the list. This occurs because the function didn't include the value in the Employee number column. This is not an error; that number should not be included in the total.

	Choose **Ignore Error**	To accept the formula as is and hide the error indicator.
9	Edit F5 to read **1000**	To change the value of the cell and the sum.
	Observe G5	The sum changed from 23442 to 16158. Functions are automatically updated when the values in their ranges are changed.
	Undo the change	Click the Undo button on the Quick Access toolbar or press Ctrl+Z.
10	Select G6	You'll enter a SUM function that contains a syntax error.
	Type **=SUM C6:F6**	To enter the function without its required parentheses.
	Press (↵ ENTER)	A Microsoft Office Excel dialog box appears, reporting an error in the function and proposing a correction.
	Click **Yes**	To accept the proposed correction. Excel adds the missing parentheses to the function.
11	Hide the error indicator in the cell	Select G6, click the Trace Error button, and choose Ignore Error.
12	Update the workbook	

Using the mouse to enter range references

Explanation

You can use the mouse to enter a range reference in a formula or function. To do so:

1 Type the equal sign, the function name, and the opening parenthesis for the function.

2 Drag to select a range for the reference.

3 Type the closing parenthesis and press Enter. Or you can enter more arguments by typing a comma (,) and continuing.

Do it!

A-2: Using the mouse to enter a function argument

Here's how	Here's why
1 Select G7	You'll enter the SUM function to calculate the sales total for Audrey Kress.
2 Type **=SUM(**	You'll use the mouse to enter the argument for this function. A ScreenTip appears below the cell.

Drag from C7 to F7, as shown

Emp #	Qtr1	Qtr2	Qtr3	Qtr4	Total
16	6354	4846	3958	8284	23442
22	7546	6574	5767	6234	26121
27	7635	4765	5256	7865	=sum(C7:F7

	As you drag, the reference for the range you're selecting appears in the function. A marquee surrounds the range you select.
Press (↵ ENTER)	Excel automatically inserts the closing parenthesis and enters the function.
Ignore the error indicator in G7	The employee number in B7 is correctly omitted from the sum.
3 Select G7	If necessary.
Observe the formula bar	

f_x	=SUM(C7:F7)

This is the function in the cell.

4 Enter the proper SUM function in G8	Use any method you like.
5 Update the workbook	

Inserting functions

Explanation

You don't need to memorize all the functions available and the arguments necessary for each function. Instead, you can use the Insert Function dialog box, which lists all of the functions. When you choose a function, Excel prompts you for required and optional arguments.

To insert a function:

1 Select the cell where you want to enter the function.
2 Click the Insert Function button on the formula bar to open the Insert Function dialog box.
3 Select a function category and a function, and click OK. Excel opens the Function Arguments dialog box that's specific to the function you're entering (as shown in Exhibit 4-3).
4 In the argument boxes, enter arguments for the function. You can use the Collapse buttons (to the right of the text boxes) to minimize the dialog box temporarily, and select cells or ranges by using the mouse.
5 Click OK.

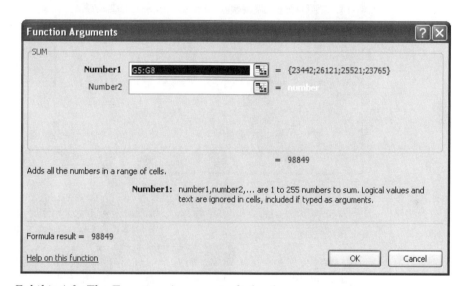

Exhibit 4-3: The Function Arguments dialog box

Do it!

A-3: Inserting a SUM function

Here's how	Here's why
1 Select G9	You'll enter a SUM function here by using the Insert Function button.
2 Click f_x	(On the formula bar.) To open the Insert Function dialog box. You'll choose a function category and a function.
3 Observe the dialog box	

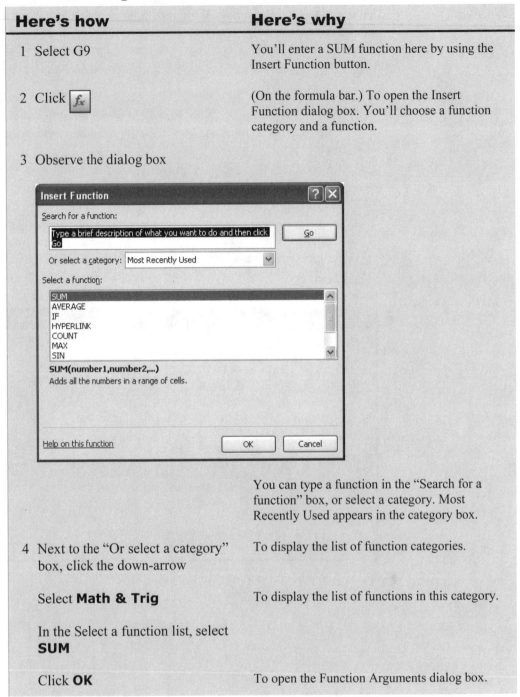

	You can type a function in the "Search for a function" box, or select a category. Most Recently Used appears in the category box.
4 Next to the "Or select a category" box, click the down-arrow	To display the list of function categories.
Select **Math & Trig**	To display the list of functions in this category.
In the Select a function list, select **SUM**	
Click **OK**	To open the Function Arguments dialog box.

5 Click as shown

Number1	G5:G8	
Number2		

To collapse the dialog box. Now you can use the mouse to enter the argument for the function.

   Select C9:F9

To select the range as the argument for the SUM function.

   Press ↵ ENTER

To enter the argument and expand the dialog box again. Notice the formula result displayed near the bottom of the dialog box.

6 Click **OK**

To insert the function and close the dialog box.

   Update the workbook

Topic B: AutoSum

Explanation

Entering references for a long range in a sum formula can be a tedious task. Excel's AutoSum feature automatically inserts the formula and arguments for a function.

The AutoSum button

When you select a cell and click the AutoSum button, Excel guesses the range of values you want to use as the argument, as shown in Exhibit 4-4 and Exhibit 4-5. For example, if you use the button at the bottom of a column of numbers, Excel assumes that the cells above the current cell should be used as the function argument. You can either accept this argument or enter your own.

Qtr1	Qtr2	Qtr3
6354	4846	3958
7546	6574	5767
7635	4765	5256
9595	5859	4879
8765	4598	5550
=SUM(C5:C9)		
SUM(number1, [number2], ...)		

Exhibit 4-4: The AutoSum function guesses at the range of data to be added

Emp #	Qtr1	Qtr2	Qtr3	Qtr4	Total	
16	6354	4846	3958	8284	=SUM(B5:F5)	
22	7546	6574	5767	6234	SUM(number1, [number2], ...)	
29	9595	5859	4879	3432	22765	

Exhibit 4-5: The guess is not always correct

Using AutoSum to enter several functions

AutoSum can also enter SUM functions at several locations simultaneously. For example, if you want to enter totals at the bottom of several columns of values, select all the cells that should contain the SUM function and click the AutoSum button. Although this process is simple and quick, you need to ensure that the cells you select for inserting the functions are correct.

Do it!

B-1: Using the AutoSum button

Here's how	Here's why
1 Select C10	You'll enter a SUM function to calculate the Qtr1 total.
Activate the Home tab	If necessary.
In the Editing group, click the down-arrow beside the AutoSum button	Σ ▾ A▾ 🔍
	Σ <u>S</u>um
	<u>A</u>verage
	<u>C</u>ount Numbers
	<u>M</u>ax
	M<u>i</u>n
	More <u>F</u>unctions...
	To display a menu that includes several common functions and provides a way to access even more.
Click anywhere on the worksheet	To close the menu.
2 Click Σ	*fx* =SUM(C5:C9)
	To automatically create a SUM function. The argument for the function is C5:C9.
Press ↵ ENTER	To enter the function.
3 Select D10:G10	To specify the range of cells that will contain the formula.
4 Click Σ	To enter SUM functions in all the selected cells.
5 Examine the formulas in D10:G10	You entered all of these formulas with a single click.
6 Update the workbook	

Topic C: Other useful functions

This topic covers the following Microsoft Certified Application Specialist exam objective for Excel 2007.

#	Objective
3.2.1	Use SUM, COUNT, COUNTA, AVERAGE, MIN, MAX
	• COUNT
	• COUNTA
	• AVERAGE
	• MIN
	• MAX

Frequently used functions in Excel

Explanation

Excel provides hundreds of functions, which range from the simple to the complex. The functions list includes frequently used functions such as AVERAGE, MIN, MAX, COUNT, and COUNTA.

The AVERAGE function

The *AVERAGE* function calculates the arithmetic mean of a list of values. The function has the following syntax:

```
=AVERAGE(number1,number2,…)
```

In this syntax, the arguments *number1* and *number2* specify the values to be used in the calculation. Commas separate each argument. The average is determined by summing the values in the arguments and then dividing that sum by the number of values. Excel does not include blank cells while calculating the average. If the ranges you specify have no values in them, AVERAGE returns an error.

Using AutoSum to enter other functions

You already know how to use the AutoSum button to enter the SUM function automatically. You can also use this button to enter other functions, such as AVERAGE, MIN, MAX, and COUNT. To do so, click the down-arrow next to the AutoSum button and select the function you want. Excel automatically specifies the range of values to be used as the function's arguments. You can either accept these arguments or enter your own.

Do it!

C-1: Using AVERAGE

Here's how	Here's why
1 Select C12	You'll enter a function here to calculate the average of the bonus sales figures for Qtr1.

Using functions**4–13**

2 Type **=AV**

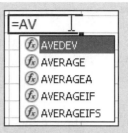

To begin entering the function to calculate the average. Excel displays a list of all functions that begin with "AV."

Double-click **AVERAGE**

To finish entering the first part of the function, up to where the arguments begin.

Select the range C5:C9

To select this range as the argument of the function.

Press (↵ ENTER)

To insert the closing parenthesis and enter the AVERAGE function.

3 Select D12

You'll calculate the average for Qtr2 sales.

In the Editing group, click the down-arrow beside the AutoSum button

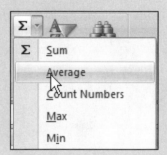

To display a menu of functions.

Choose **Average**

Excel automatically takes C12 as the argument for the function, because it is the only adjacent value.

Select D5:D9

To select this range as the argument of the function. A marquee appears around D5:D9.

Press (↵ ENTER)

To enter the function. The average of the Qtr2 sales appears.

4 Copy the function in D12 to E12:F12

Use any method you like.

5 Update the workbook

The MIN function

Explanation

The *MIN* function returns the smallest number from a list of values. This function has the following syntax:

```
=MIN(number1,number2,…)
```

Arguments for this function can include numbers, empty cells, logical values, or text representations of numbers (such as dates). Error values or text that can't be translated into numbers will cause an error.

Do it!

C-2:   Using MIN

Here's how	Here's why
1 Select C13	You'll enter a function here to return the lowest Qtr1 value.
2 Type **=M**	To display a list of functions that begin with the letter M.
Select **MIN**	(Double-click MIN in the list that appears.) The MIN function returns the lowest value (the minimum) in the list of values specified as its argument.
Select C5:C9	To select this range as the argument of the function.
Press (↵ ENTER)	
3 Copy the formula in C13 to D13:F13	
4 Update the workbook	

The MAX function

Explanation

The *MAX* function returns the largest number in a list of values and has the following syntax:

```
=MAX(number1,[number2],…)
```

Exhibit 4-6 shows the results of the MAX function for each quarter.

Name	Emp #	Qtr1	Qtr2	Qtr3	Qtr4	Total
		Outlander Spices				
		Bonus sales for the northern region				
Kendra James	16	6354	4846	3958	8284	23442
Alan Monder	22	7546	6574	5767	6234	26121
Audrey Kress	27	7635	4765	5256	7865	25521
Julie George	29	9595	5859	4879	3432	23765
James Overmire	42	8765	4598	5550	4876	23789
Totals		39895	26642	25410	30691	122638
Average		7979	5328.4	5082	6138.2	
Minimum		6354	4598	3958	3432	
Maximum		9595	6574	5767	8284	

Exhibit 4-6: Average, minimum, and maximum values

Do it!

C-3:   Using MAX

Here's how	Here's why
1 Select C14	You'll enter a function that will return the largest Qtr1 value.
2 Enter the first part of the **MAX** function	(Type =M and then double-click MAX in the list.) MAX is the function that returns the largest value (the maximum) in a list of values.
Select C5:C9	
Press (↵ ENTER)	
3 Copy the formula in C14 to D14:F14	
4 Deselect the range	Compare your work to Exhibit 4-6.
5 Update the workbook	

The COUNT and COUNTA functions

Explanation

You can use the COUNT function to determine how many cells in a range contain numeric values. The COUNT function will recognize only cells that contain numbers; it will not count any cells that are blank or that contain text.

The syntax for COUNT is:

```
=COUNT(value1, value2,…)
```

The COUNTA function will count not only how many cells in a range contain numbers, but also how many cells contain text. COUNTA will not, however, include blank cells in the count. The syntax for the COUNTA function is:

```
=COUNTA(value1, value2,…)
```

Do it!

C-4: Using COUNT and COUNTA

Here's how	Here's why
1 Select C16	You'll determine the total number of Quarterly sales figures for the year.
2 Enter the first part of the COUNT function	To begin the formula.
Select C4:F9	To specify the range of cells to count.
Press (↵ ENTER)	To complete the formula and return the result of 20. Note that even though you included C4:F4 in the range, those cells were not counted toward the total because they don't contain numeric values.
3 Select C17	You'll use COUNTA to count the number of northern region employees involved in the quarterly sales.
4 Enter the first part of the COUNTA function	
Select A5:A9	To specify the range to count.
Press (↵ ENTER)	To complete the formula and return the result of 5. COUNTA will count all non-empty cells.
5 Undo the action	You'll enter a different range in the formula to determine the same result.
6 In C17, enter the first part of the COUNTA function	
Select B5:B11	
Press (↵ ENTER)	To return the result of 5. COUNTA ignores empty cells.
7 Update and close the workbook	

Unit summary: Using functions

Topic A

In this topic, you learned that **functions** are predefined formulas you can use to perform specific types of calculations. You learned that all functions consist of an equal sign, the name of the function, and **arguments** enclosed in parentheses. You learned how to use the **SUM function** to add a list of values. You learned how to **trace errors**, and you learned that Excel will attempt to correct **syntax errors**. You also learned how to enter a function's arguments by typing and by using the mouse. In addition, you learned how to use the **Insert Function** dialog box to enter a function.

Topic B

In this topic, you learned how to use the **AutoSum** button. You learned that you can use AutoSum to enter a SUM function quickly, either in a single cell or in a range.

Topic C

In this topic, you learned how to use **AVERAGE** to calculate the average of a list of values, use **MIN** to calculate the lowest value in a list, and use **MAX** to calculate the highest value in a list. You also used **COUNT** and **COUNTA** to determine the number of cells in a selection.

Independent practice activity

In this activity, you will enter functions to display the sum, average, minimum, and maximum of values. You'll also enter the result of a COUNT function.

1 Open Practice function and save it as **My practice function**. This workbook contains home-run statistics for the Outlander company softball team.

2 In B21, enter a function to calculate Bill MacArthur's total number of home runs.

3 In B22, enter a function to calculate Bill's average number of home runs per year.

4 In B23, enter a function to calculate his lowest number of home runs in a year.

5 In B24, enter a function to calculate Bill's highest number of home runs in a year.

6 In B25, enter a function to count the number of years Bill has been hitting home runs.

7 In G6, enter a formula to calculate how many home runs Bill needs to hit to tie Michael Lee's record. (*Hint:* This will be the difference between the values in cells G5 and B21. For example, the difference between the values in B10 and B15 would be written as =B10-B15.)

8 Compare your work to Exhibit 4-7.

9 Update and close the workbook.

	A	B	C	D	E	F	G
1	Outlander company softball team						
2	Home runs by Bill MacArthur by year						
3							
4	Year	Home runs					
5	1992	3			Michael Lee's record total:		175
6	1993	8			HR MacArthur needs to tie:		22
7	1994	16					
8	1995	10					
9	1996	7					
10	1997	2					
11	1998	14					
12	1999	9					
13	2000	9					
14	2001	19					
15	2002	18					
16	2003	12					
17	2004	10					
18	2005	7					
19	2006	9					
20							
21	Total	153					
22	Average	10.2					
23	Low	2					
24	High	19					
25	# of Years	15					

Exhibit 4-7: The workbook's appearance after Step 7 of the independent practice activity

Review questions

1 What is a function?

2 When there might be an error in a cell, Excel's error-checking feature warns you by displaying an error indicator. What does this indicator look like and where does it appear?

3 What is the syntax for the SUM function?

4 Which function is used to calculate the arithmetic mean of a list of values?

5 If your worksheet contains total sales figures for each of your salespeople, which function could you use to find the salesperson with the highest sales?

6 Which function would you use to count the total number of sales transactions in a given time period?

Unit 5

Formatting worksheets

Unit time: 60 minutes

Complete this unit, and you'll know how to:

A Format text to use different fonts, sizes, and styles.

B Change column widths, row heights, and alignment, and apply formatting to all cells in a row.

C Format values as currency, percentages, or ordinary numbers.

D Use conditional formats based on specific criteria.

E Copy formats, and use cell styles and table styles to apply formats.

Topic A: Formatting text

This topic covers the following Microsoft Certified Application Specialist exam objective for Excel 2007.

#	Objective
2.3.4	**Format text in cells**
	• Font, alignment, attributes, wrapping, etc.

Working with text in cells

Explanation

You can format text by changing its font, size, style, and color. You can format all the text in the active cell or only a selected portion of the text. In addition, you can select multiple cells and apply formatting to all of them at once.

The Font group

Although there are several ways to format cells, one of the most efficient techniques is to activate the Home tab and use the Font group, shown in Exhibit 5-1. This group provides tools for commonly used formatting options.

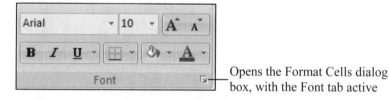

Opens the Format Cells dialog box, with the Font tab active

Exhibit 5-1: Formatting options in the Font group

The following table lists the buttons in the Font group.

Button	Button name
Arial ▾	Font
10 ▾	Font Size
A▴	Increase Font Size
A▾	Decrease Font Size
B	Bold
I	Italic
U ▾	Underline
A ▾	Font Color
◇ ▾	Fill Color
▦ ▾	Borders

To format cells by using the Font group, select the cell or range you want to format, and click the formatting button you want. You can select a font and size from the drop-down lists.

Do it!

A-1: Using the Font group to format text

Here's how	Here's why
1 Open Formatting	(In the current unit folder.) The data in this workbook is difficult to read because there is no formatting.
2 Save the workbook as **My formatting**	In the current unit folder.
3 Select A6:B6	You'll make these headings stand out by changing their formatting.
Activate the Home tab	If necessary.
Click ⊞ **B**	(The Bold button is in the Font group.) To make the headings in A6:B6 bold.
4 Select C6:F6	To select the heading titles for the quarterly sales figures.
Click ⊞ *I*	(The Italic button is in the Font group.) To make the Qtr headings italic.
5 Select A1	You'll make the title text larger and change the font.
In the Font group, click the Font Size down-arrow as shown	
	To display a list of font sizes.
Select **16**, as shown	
	To increase the size of the text to 16 points.

6 Click the Font list down-arrow	(In the Font group.) To display the Font list.
Move the pointer down the list of fonts, while observing the text in A1	The selected text changes to show what it would look like in each font.
Choose **Arial Black**	
7 Make A2 italic	Select the cell and click the Italic button.
8 Update the workbook	

Non-contiguous ranges

Explanation

The same formatting can be applied to cells that are not adjacent to each other. For example, you might want to apply a specific format to cells A1 and B4 and the range C6:D7. To do this, you can select them as a *non-contiguous range*—a range of cells located in non-adjacent areas of the worksheet.

To select a non-contiguous range, select the first cell or range. Then hold the Ctrl key and select other cells or ranges you want to include. This non-contiguous range can then be formatted as you would format any other selection.

Do it!

A-2:   Formatting non-contiguous ranges

Here's how	Here's why
1 Select G4	To select the first of the three non-contiguous ranges. You'll apply bold formatting to G4, A11, and G6:H6 in a single step.
Press and hold `CTRL`	
While holding `CTRL`, select A11	To add A11 to the selection.
Select G6:H6	To select all three ranges.
Release `CTRL`	
2 Click **B**	To apply bold formatting to the selected non-contiguous ranges.
Deselect the range	(Click any cell.) To see the formatting you applied.
3 Update the workbook	

The Format Cells dialog box

Explanation

The Format Cells dialog box provides a variety of formatting options. Its Font tab (shown in Exhibit 5-2) is used to select font, style, size, and other options.

Exhibit 5-2: The Font tab in the Format Cells dialog box

Here's how to use the Format Cells dialog box to format cells:

1 Select the cell or range you want to format.

2 Right-click and choose Format Cells to open the Format Cells dialog box.

3 Activate the Font tab.

4 Select the desired formatting. You can see what the formatted cells will look like in the Preview box. Then, click OK.

Do it!   **A-3:   Using the Format Cells dialog box to format text**

Here's how	Here's why
1 Select A1	You'll change the font and size of the worksheet title.
2 Right-click the selection	To display a shortcut menu.
Choose **Format Cells...**	To open the Format Cells dialog box.
Activate the Font tab	If necessary.
3 From the Font list, select **Times New Roman**	You'll need to scroll the Font list to find it.
From the Font style list, select **Bold Italic**	
From the Size list, select **18**	

Font:	Font style:	Size:
Times New Roman	Bold Italic	18
Tall Paul	Regular	12
Tempus Sans ITC	Italic	14
Terminal	Bold	16
Times New Roman	Bold Italic	18
Trebuchet MS		20
Tunga		22

	The Preview box on the Font tab shows how the text will look with this formatting.
4 Click **OK**	To apply the formatting to the cell.
5 Select A2	
Make the text **Times New Roman**, **12** point	*Outlander Spices*
	Bonus sales for the northern region
	(Use the Format Cells dialog box.) The title and subtitle should look like this.
6 Update the workbook	

Topic B: Formatting rows and columns

This topic covers the following Microsoft Certified Application Specialist exam objectives for Excel 2007.

#	Objective
1.3.1	**Cut, copy, and paste data and cell contents**
	• Paste data from a bordered cell without pasting borders
2.2.2	**Format rows and columns**
	• Format all the cells in a row or column simultaneously
2.2.4	**Modify row height and column width**
	• Using AutoFit
	• Using a specified value
2.3.4	**Format text in cells**
	• Font, alignment, attributes, wrapping, etc.
2.3.7	**Add and remove cell borders**

Applying formatting to rows and columns

Explanation

You can apply various formats, such as borders and alignment, to enhance the appearance of one or more cells in a row or column. You can also adjust the cell height and width. However, this change affects an entire row or column. You cannot change the height or width of an individual cell.

Changing column widths and row heights

Excel automatically adjusts row height to accommodate the size of data in a row. Column widths typically need to be adjusted manually. Here are some methods for changing column widths:

- **Drag the column border.** When you point to the border between two column headings, the pointer becomes a two-headed arrow. You can then drag the border to the left or right to decrease or increase the column width.

- **Double-click the column border.** This automatically sizes the column to fit the widest data it contains.

- **Set a specific column size in numbers.** To do this, you select a column, right-click, choose Column Width, enter a number, and click OK.

The same methods work for changing the row height.

Using AutoFit

You can use the AutoFit feature to automatically adjust column widths and row heights. To use this feature, you select the column or row, display the Format menu in the Cells group, and choose the appropriate AutoFit option.

Setting the width of multiple columns

To set several contiguous columns to the same width, select the columns and then use one of the methods above to change the width. This works for setting row height, too.

Do it!

B-1: Changing column width and row height

Here's how	Here's why
1 Select A1	The employee names and the date in column A do not fit in the column. Excel truncates the data, so you can't see all of it.
2 Point to the border between the column headings A and B	The pointer changes to a two-headed arrow.
Press and hold the mouse button, and drag slightly to the right, to the column width indicated	As you drag, the new column width appears in a ScreenTip.
Release the mouse button	To resize the column. Now you can see more of the employee names, but the date in A4 still isn't visible.
3 Widen the column until all the data is visible	Point to the border between column headings A and B, drag to the right until the ScreenTip shows a width of approximately 14.5 points, and then release the mouse button.

4	Select column B	You'll automatically size the column to fit the widest data it contains.
	In the Cells group, click **Format**	To display the Format menu.
	Choose **AutoFit Column Width**	To resize the column to fit the data. In this case, the column width decreases.
5	Select columns C:F	(Drag over their column headings.) You'll resize these columns in one step.
6	Right-click the selection	To display a shortcut menu.
	Choose **Column Width...**	To open the Column Width dialog box.
7	In the Column width box, type **7**	To specify that the selected columns should be seven characters wide.
	Click **OK**	To change the width of the selected columns.
8	Select row 2	Click the row-2 heading button.
9	Right-click the selection	To display the shortcut menu.
	Choose **Row Height...**	To open the Row Height dialog box.
	Type **20**	To specify the row height as 20 points.
	Click **OK**	To change the height of the selected row.
10	Deselect the row	
11	Update the workbook	

Applying a fill color to a row or column

In addition to changing the row height or column width, you can apply formats such as fill color to entire rows or columns simultaneously. To apply a fill color to several rows at once, select the rows. Activate the Home tab, click the arrow next to the Fill Color button in the Font group to open a color palette, and then choose your desired color.

Do it!

B-2:   Applying color to a row

Here's how	Here's why
1 Select row 6	
2 On the Home tab, in the Font group, click as shown	Click the down-arrow on the Fill Color button to open the color palette.
3 In the palette, select a light green color	The chosen color is applied to all cells in the row.
Apply the same fill color to row 16	Select the row and click the Fill Color button.
Deselect the row	
4 Update the workbook	

Using alignment options

Explanation   *Alignment* in Excel refers to the location of data within a cell. For example, the data you type can be aligned horizontally to appear in the left, right, or center area of a cell. The data can be aligned vertically to appear at the top, bottom, or middle of the cell. By default, text aligns to the left and bottom of the cell, while values align to the right and bottom. To align the contents of a cell or range, select the cell or range, activate the Home tab, and click one of the buttons in the Alignment group, shown in Exhibit 5-3.

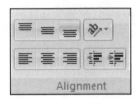

Exhibit 5-3: The alignment buttons in the Alignment group

The following table lists the buttons in the Alignment group.

Button	Button name
	Align Left
	Center
	Align Right
	Top Align
	Middle Align
	Bottom Align

The Merge & Center button

The Merge & Center button centers data over a range of cells (instead of within a single column). To use it, select the cell containing the data to merge and center, and select the rest of the cells over which you want to center the data. Activate the Home tab. Then, in the Alignment group, click Merge & Center. For example, to center the text in B1 over columns A:F, select A1:F1 and click Merge & Center.

Do it!

B-3: Setting alignment

Here's how	Here's why
1 Select B6:H6	You'll center the text over the columns.
Click ▤	(The Center button is in the Alignment group.) To center the text within the cells.
2 Select G4	This text is truncated. You'll change its alignment so that it is completely visible.
Click ▤	(The Align Right button is in the Alignment group.) To right-align the text in the cell. The part of the data that doesn't fit seems to be showing in the cell to the left, F4.
3 Select A1:H1	You'll center the worksheet title "Outlander Spices" over all of these cells.
Click ▤	(The Merge & Center button is in the Alignment group.) To center the text in A1 over the entire range.
4 Center the text in A2 over A2:H2	(Select A2:H2 and click the Merge & Center button.) To center the Bonus sales subheading over this entire range.
5 Deselect the range	There are no column border gridlines in the ranges A1:H1 or A2:H2. When you use the Merge & Center button, the selected range becomes a single cell.
6 Select A2:H2	(Click anywhere in the new single cell.) You'll change the vertical alignment of the cell.
Click ▤	(The Middle Align button is in the Alignment group.) To align the text in the middle of the cell.
Observe the cell	

	B	C	D	E	F
	Outlander Spices				
	Bonus sales for the northern region				

The Bonus sales subheading now appears in the vertical middle of the cell.

7 Update the workbook

Applying borders

Explanation

Click the Borders button in the Font group to display a menu of border styles that you can apply to cells or ranges. The menu is shown in Exhibit 5-4. For more options, choose More Borders to open the Format Cells dialog box.

The Borders tab in the Format Cells dialog box is shown in Exhibit 5-5. This tab provides more options than the Borders menu.

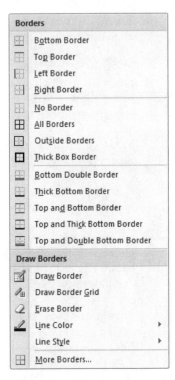

Exhibit 5-4: The Borders menu

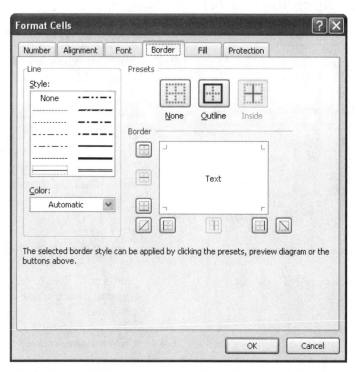

Exhibit 5-5: The Border tab in the Format Cells dialog box

Do it!

B-4: Applying borders to ranges

Here's how	Here's why
1 Select A6:H6	You'll put a heavy border below this text to separate it from the data below.
2 Click as shown	 (The Borders button is in the Font group.) To display the Borders menu.
Select **Thick Bottom Border**	
Deselect the range	You can now see the border you just applied.
3 Select A10:H10	You'll put a light border below this range to separate the individual employee data from the totals row.
4 Display the Borders menu	Click the arrow beside the Borders button.
Choose **More Borders...**	To open the Format Cells dialog box with the Border tab active.
Under Line, in the Style box, click as shown	 To select the dashed line.
5 Click	 (Under Border.) To make the dashed line a border for the bottom of the selected range.
Click **OK**	To apply the border and close the dialog box.

6 Deselect the range	To see the new border.
7 Update the workbook	

Applying borders by using the border-drawing pencil

Explanation

You can also draw borders around cells or ranges by using the border-drawing pencil. To do so:

1 Click the Borders button in the Font group to display the Borders menu.
2 Choose Draw Border, or choose a line color and line style. The pointer changes to a drawing pencil.
3 Drag where you want to apply a border.

Do it!

B-5:   Using the border-drawing pencil

Here's how	Here's why
1 Display the Borders menu	You'll draw a border below a range of values.
Under Draw Borders, choose **Line Style**	To display the Line Style gallery.
2 Select the indicated style	
3 Observe the pointer	It changes to a pencil.
4 Drag the pencil under A4	To draw a border under this value.
Update the workbook	Notice that when you update the workbook, the pointer changes back to its original shape.

Pasting bordered data without pasting borders

Explanation

You can copy and paste data in a bordered cell without pasting the border. To do so, you can either:

- Copy the bordered cell or range. Select the destination cell, display the Paste menu in the Clipboard group, and choose No Borders.
- Copy the bordered cell or range. Select the destination cell and right-click it. From the shortcut menu, choose Paste Special. In the Paste Special dialog box, under Paste, select All except borders, and click OK.

Do it!

B-6:   Using the Paste Special option

Here's how	Here's why
1 Copy A4	
2 Select A24 as the destination cell	
Right-click A24	To display the shortcut menu.
3 Choose **Paste Special...**	To open the Paste Special dialog box.
Under Paste, select **All except borders**	To remove the border when the value is pasted.
Click **OK**	To close the dialog box and paste the value. The border in A4 is not pasted in A24.
4 Update the workbook	

Removing borders

Explanation

When you no longer want a border on a cell or range, you can remove it. Select the cell or range containing the border you want to remove. Then, from the Borders menu, choose No Border.

Do it!

B-7:   Removing a border

Here's how	Here's why
1 Select A4	You'll delete the border from this cell.
2 Display the Borders menu and choose **No Border**	To remove the borders from the selected cell.
3 Deselect the cell	The border is deleted.
Update the workbook	

Topic C: Formatting numbers

This topic covers the following Microsoft Certified Application Specialist exam objective for Excel 2007.

#	Objective
2.3.1	**Apply number formats** • Format the values in the cell with a specified number of decimal places • Format the values in the cell as a date

Number formats

Explanation

Numbers, including date and time, can be displayed in many different formats. The actual cell value is not affected when you apply number formatting.

The Number group

Dollar signs ($), percent signs (%), and the number of decimal places are examples of number formatting. By using number formats, you can make your worksheets easier to understand and call attention to specific data. The Number group, shown in Exhibit 5-6, provides several tools for formatting numbers.

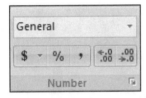

Exhibit 5-6: Number formatting options in the Number group

Button	Button name
$ ▾	Accounting Number Format
%	Percent Style
,	Comma Style
←.0 .00	Increase Decimal
.00 →.0	Decrease Decimal

Sometimes number formatting will make the data too wide to be displayed at the current column width. When this happens, Excel displays a series of number signs (#) instead of a truncated number. (This is done because the visible part of a truncated number might be mistaken for the complete number.) If number signs are displayed, either increase the column width or change the formatting of the number.

11/27/2006 11:51						Comm_rate:	4%
Name	**Emp #**	*Qtr1*	*Qtr2*	*Qtr3*	*Qtr4*	**Total**	**Comm**
Kendra James	16	6354	4846	3958	8284	$ 23,458	$ 938
Alan Monder	22	7546	6574	5767	6234	$ 26,143	$ 1,046
Audrey Kress	27	7635	4765	5256	7865	$ 25,548	$ 1,022
Julie George	29	9595	5859	4879	3432	$ 23,794	$ 952
Totals		$ 31,130	$ 22,044	$ 19,860	$ 25,815	$ 98,943	$ 3,958
Bonus sales for the southern region							
Name	Emp #	Qtr1	Qtr2	Qtr3	Qtr4	Total	Comm
Michael Bobrow	16	5493	8732	7722	3990	25953	1038.12
Karen Anderson	22	8765	3224	8865	4936	25812	1032.48
James Hanover	27	3440	3958	5784	4601	17810	712.4
Kelly Palmatier	29	3716	8917	5662	3324	21648	865.92
Totals		21414	24831	28033	16851	91223	3648.92

Exhibit 5-7: The number formatting applied in the next activity

Do it!

C-1: Using the Number group to format numbers

Here's how	Here's why
1 Select G7:H10	You'll format the numbers in these cells as currency.
While holding (CTRL), select C11:H11	
2 Click as shown	
	Accounting Number Format
	(The Accounting Number Format button is in the Number group.) To display the Currency gallery.
3 Select **$ English (U.S.)**	To format the numbers in G7:H11 as currency with two decimal places and with a comma separating the thousands place. C11:F11 show number signs (#) because the data is too wide to fit in the cells.
4 Click [.00/.0] twice	(The Decrease Decimal button is in the Number group.) To decrease the number of decimal places from two to zero. The numbers in C11:F11 are still too wide to be displayed.
5 Select columns C:H	(Drag over the column headings.) You'll size the columns to fit the contents.
6 Point to the right border of the heading for column H, as shown	
	The pointer changes to a double-headed arrow.
Double-click the right border	The columns resize to fit the largest item in each.
7 Select H4	The commission rate should be a percentage.
Click [%]	To apply the percentage format to the cell.
8 Observe the various number formats in the worksheet	As shown in Exhibit 5-7.
9 Update the workbook	

The Format Cells dialog box

Explanation

The Number tab in the Format Cells dialog box offers a variety of number formats, including dates, times, fractions, and scientific notation, as shown in Exhibit 5-8. To open the Format Cells dialog box with the Number tab activated, click the Dialog Box Launcher button in the Number group on the Ribbon.

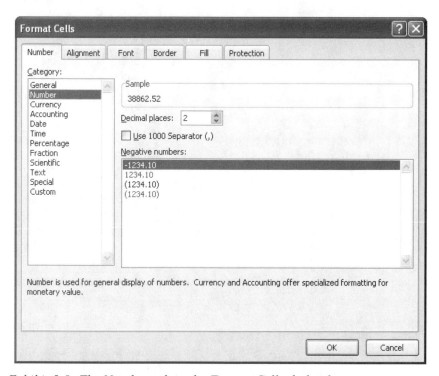

Exhibit 5-8: The Number tab in the Format Cells dialog box

Do it!

C-2: Exploring the Number tab

Here's how	Here's why
1 Select A4	This cell uses a NOW function to return the current date and time. You'll view some number formats and change the format of this date.
2 In the Number group, click ⬚	(The Dialog Box Launcher is in the bottom-right corner of the group.) To open the Format Cells dialog box with the Number tab activated. Here, you can select a number format category. When the category is selected, other options become available.
3 From the Category list, select **Number**	The dialog box will resemble Exhibit 5-8. For numbers, you can specify the number of decimal places and whether to display a comma as a thousands separator. You can also specify how you want negative numbers to appear.
4 From the Category list, select **Currency**	Currency formats give you the option of choosing a currency symbol.
Click the Symbol down-arrow, as shown	Symbol: None ▾ / Negative numbers: To display a list of currency symbol choices.
5 From the Category list, select **Fraction**	Up to one digit (1/4) / Up to two digits (21/25) / Up to three digits (312/943) / As halves (1/2) / As quarters (2/4) / As eighths (4/8) / As sixteenths (8/16) To display the decimal value of a number as a fraction.

6 From the Category list, select **Date**

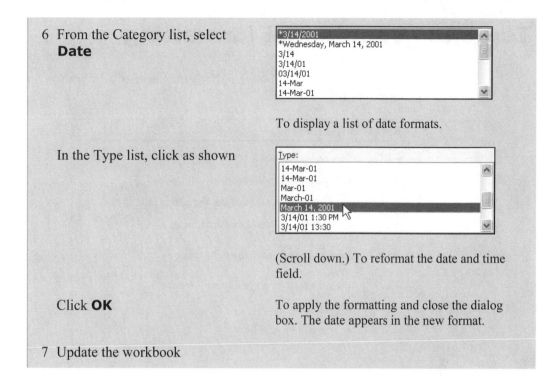

To display a list of date formats.

In the Type list, click as shown

(Scroll down.) To reformat the date and time field.

Click **OK**

To apply the formatting and close the dialog box. The date appears in the new format.

7 Update the workbook

Topic D: Conditional formatting

This topic covers the following Microsoft Certified Application Specialist exam objectives for Excel 2007.

#	Objective
4.3.1	**Manage conditional formats by using the rule manager** • Create a new conditional formatting rule • Edit an existing conditional formatting rule • Delete a conditional formatting rule
4.3.2	**Allow more than one rule to be true**
4.3.3	**Apply the following conditional formats:** • Highlight • Top, bottom rules

Working with conditional formatting

Explanation

Conditional formatting is applied to data only if one or more specific conditions are satisfied. You can use a different color or format to highlight the values satisfying a specific condition. For example, you can highlight in green all sales figures that exceed $75,000. Conditional formatting can be applied based on a cell value or a formula.

Creating conditional formats

To conditionally format data:

1 Select the cell or range containing the values to which you want to apply conditional formatting.

2 In the Styles group, click Conditional Formatting.

3 Do one of the following:

- Choose a condition and rule from the menu, shown in Exhibit 5-9.

- Choose New Rule. Then, specify a condition and format in the New Formatting Rule dialog box, shown in Exhibit 5-10.

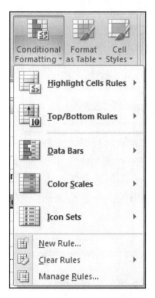

Exhibit 5-9: The Conditional Formatting menu

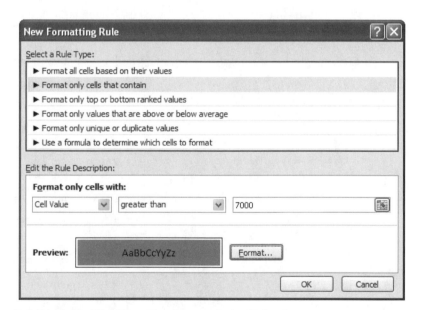

Exhibit 5-10: The New Formatting Rule dialog box

Do it!

D-1:   Creating a conditional format

Here's how	Here's why
1 Select C7:F10	You'll apply a conditional format that will highlight values if they're less than 4000.
2 In the Styles group, click **Conditional Formatting**	To display the Conditional Formatting menu.
Choose **Highlight Cells Rules**, **Less Than...**	To open the Less Than dialog box.

3 In the first box, type **4000**

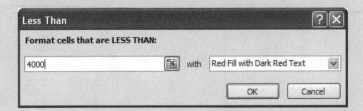

Press `TAB`	To move the insertion point to the fill list.
4 Observe the range	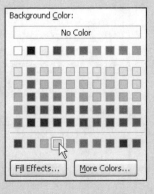

Excel displays a preview of the formatting. Two cells that meet the condition are highlighted with a red fill and red text.

From the fill list, select **Custom Format...**	To open the Format Cells dialog box.
Activate the Fill tab	You'll change the fill to yellow.
5 In the Background Color palette, select as shown	

Click **OK**	To apply the color and close the Format Cells dialog box.
Observe the range	The preview now displays a yellow fill in the cells that meet the condition.
6 Click **OK**	To apply the conditional format and close the Less Than dialog box.
Deselect the range	E7 and F10 appear in yellow because the values they contain are less than 4000.
7 In D9, enter **3500**	To change Audrey Kress's Qtr2 sales figure. The cell now has a yellow fill.

8 Select C7:F10 again	You'll create a conditional format to highlight sales figures greater than 7000.
Click **Conditional Formatting** and choose **Manage Rules...**	To open the Conditional Formatting Rules Manager. You'll create a rule by using the Rules Manager.
Click **New Rule**	To open the New Formatting Rule dialog box.
9 From the Select a Rule Type list, select **Format only cells that contain**	
Under Edit the Rule Description, in the second box, select **greater than**	
In the third box, enter **7000**	
10 Under Preview, click **Format**	To open the Format Cells dialog box. Here you can choose a color to highlight cells with values matching your condition.
In the Background Color palette, select a blue color	
Click **OK**	To close the Format Cells dialog box. The New Formatting Rule dialog box should look similar to Exhibit 5-10.
11 Click **OK**	To create the new rule and close the Conditional Formatting Rules Manager dialog box.
12 Deselect the range	Cells with a value greater than 7000 are highlighted in light blue.
13 Select G7:G10	(If necessary.) You'll highlight the top two earners.
Display the Conditional Formatting menu	
Choose **Top/Bottom Rules, Top 10 Items...**	To open the Top 10 Items dialog box.
In the first box, enter **2**	
14 Click **OK**	To close the dialog box and apply the default formatting to the top two totals in the column.
Deselect the range	The totals for Alan Monder and Audrey Kress are highlighted, making it easy to see who the top two earners are.
Update the workbook	

Modifying conditional formatting rules

Explanation

You can use the Rules Manager to edit or delete conditional formatting rules. To do so, display the Conditional Formatting menu in the Styles group, choose Manage Rules to open the Rules Manager dialog box, and select the rule you want to modify or delete.

Do it!   ## D-2: Editing and deleting a conditional format

Here's how	Here's why
1 Display the Conditional Formatting menu and choose **Manage Rules...**	To open the Conditional Formatting Rules Manager dialog box.
2 From the "Show formatting rules for" list, select **This Worksheet**	To display all the rules in effect for the current worksheet.
3 From the list of rules, select **Top 2**	You'll edit the condition to display a border.
Click **Edit Rule**	To open the Edit Formatting Rule dialog box.
4 Under Edit the Rule Description, click **Format**	To open the Format Cells dialog box.
Activate the Border tab	
Click as shown	
5 Click **OK**	To close the Format Cells dialog box.
Click **OK**	To close the Edit Formatting Rule dialog box.
Click **OK**	To close the Conditional Formatting Rules Manager and apply the new formatting.
6 Open the Conditional Formatting Rules Manager	(Choose Manage Rules from the Conditional Formatting menu.) You'll delete a rule.
Show the formatting rules for the current worksheet	From the "Show formatting rules for" list, select This Worksheet.
7 From the list of rules, select **Top 2**	
Click **Delete Rule**	To delete the rule.
Click **OK**	To close the Conditional Formatting Rules Manager and apply the change.
8 Update the workbook	

Topic E: Copying formats and applying table formats

This topic covers the following Microsoft Certified Application Specialist exam objectives for Excel 2007.

#	Objective
1.1.1	**Fill a series**
	• Fill a series with formatting only
2.3.3	**Apply and modify cell styles**
	• Format cells by using Quick Styles
	• Format cells by using other methods
2.4.1	**Apply Quick Styles to tables**
	• Apply and change Quick Styles
4.6.1	**Sort data by using single or multiple criteria**

Other methods of applying formats

Explanation

Excel provides several other formatting features, such as the Format Painter, cell styles, and table formats. You can also use the Find and Replace dialog box to change formatting.

Copying and clearing formats

Formats can be copied from one cell to another, just as values can. To copy formats:

1 Select the cell that has the formatting you want to copy.
2 Activate the Home tab (if necessary).
3 In the Clipboard group, click Format Painter to copy the selection's formatting.
4 Select the cell or range to which you want to copy the formatting.

Exhibit 5-11 shows the formatting from one set of data copied to another set of data.

To clear formatting, select the cell or range from which you want to remove the formatting. In the Editing group, click the down-arrow beside the Clear button and choose Clear Formats.

Outlander Spices
Bonus sales for the northern region

Name	Emp #	Qtr1	Qtr2	Qtr3	Qtr4	Total	Comm
November 27, 2006						Comm_rate:	4%
Name	Emp #	Qtr1	Qtr2	Qtr3	Qtr4	Total	Comm
Kendra James	16	6354	4846	3958	8284	$ 23,458	$ 938
Alan Monder	22	7546	6574	5767	6234	$ 26,143	$ 1,046
Audrey Kress	27	7635	3500	5256	7865	$ 24,283	$ 971
Julie George	29	9595	5859	4879	3432	$ 23,794	$ 952
Totals		$ 31,130	$ 20,779	$ 19,860	$ 25,815	$ 97,678	$ 3,907

Bonus sales for the southern region

Name	Emp #	Qtr1	Qtr2	Qtr3	Qtr4	Total	Comm
Michael Bobrow	16	5493	8732	7722	3990	$ 25,953	$ 1,038
Karen Anderson	22	8765	3224	8865	4936	$ 25,812	$ 1,032
James Hanover	27	3440	3958	5784	4601	$ 17,810	$ 712
Kelly Palmatier	29	3716	8917	5662	3324	$ 21,648	$ 866
Totals		$ 21,414	$ 24,831	$ 28,033	$ 16,851	$ 91,223	$ 3,649

Exhibit 5-11: The My formatting workbook with the southern region formatted

Do it!

E-1:   Copying formats

Here's how	Here's why
1 Select A2	You'll apply the formatting of this cell to A14.
Click 🖌	(The Format Painter button is in the Clipboard group.) To copy the formatting of the selected cell.
Select A14	To paste the copied formatting onto A14. The text is now formatted correctly as a region subheading.
2 Copy the formatting for the entire northern region to the southern region data	Select A6:H11, click Format Painter, and select A16:H21.
3 Deselect the range	The worksheet should resemble Exhibit 5-11.
4 Update the workbook	

Using AutoFill to copy formats

In addition to using Format Painter, you can use AutoFill to copy a format from one cell to another. To copy formatting by using AutoFill:

1 Select the cell containing the format you want to copy.

2 Drag the fill handle in the bottom-right corner of the cell over the adjacent cells whose formatting you want to change.

3 Click Auto Fill Options and choose Fill Formatting Only.

Do it!

E-2: Using AutoFill to copy a format

Here's how	Here's why
1 Select B6	You'll copy only the formatting from this cell.
2 Drag the fill handle over C6:F6	The Emp # value is copied, along with the formatting.
3 Click as shown	To display the Auto Fill Options menu.
4 From the menu, choose **Fill Formatting Only**	To restore the original data but copy the formatting from B6.
5 Update and close the workbook	

Using cell styles and table formats

Explanation

Cell styles and table formats are predefined combinations of text formats, number formats, borders, colors, and shading that you can apply in a single step. Cell styles are intended to be applied to a single cell or range. Table formats work best on data that is arranged in a table. Both cell styles and table formats use Excel 2007's Live Preview feature to show you how your cells or table will look.

To apply a cell style:

1   Select a cell or range.

2   In the Styles group, click Cell Styles.

3   Move the pointer over the styles in the gallery, shown in Exhibit 5-12. As you do, each style is previewed in the cells you selected.

4   Click a style to select it.

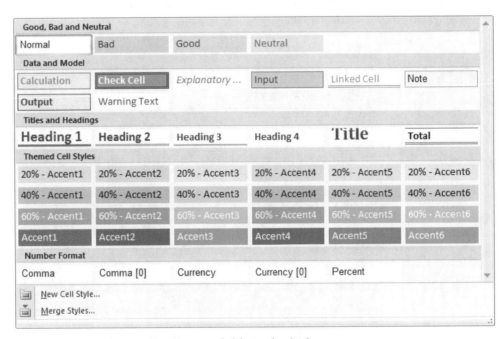

Exhibit 5-12: Built-in cell styles available in the Styles group

To apply a table format:

1 Select a cell or range.

2 In the Styles group, click Format As Table.

3 Select one of the built-in table formats (shown in Exhibit 5-13). The Format As Table dialog box appears.

4 Enter the range of the table (if necessary), and click OK. The Table Tools tab is activated.

5 In the lower-right corner of the Table Styles group, click the More button.

6 Move the pointer over the styles in the gallery. As you do, the table is shown in the style you selected.

7 Choose a table format.

8 Edit the Style Options and other group properties on the Ribbon, if necessary.

9 Click anywhere in the worksheet to close the Table Tools tab and activate the Home tab.

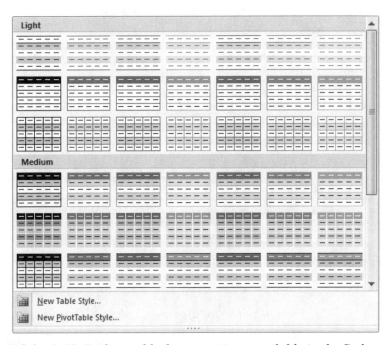

Exhibit 5-13: Built-in table format options available in the Styles group

Do it!

E-3:   Applying cell and table styles

Here's how	Here's why
1 Open Format as table	(From the current unit folder.) This workbook contains data identical to what you've seen earlier in this unit, but without any formatting applied.
2 Save the workbook as **My format as table**	
3 Select A1	You'll view cell styles and apply one to this cell.
4 In the Styles group, click **Cell Styles**	A gallery of built-in cell styles appears, as shown in Exhibit 5-12.
Move the pointer over the cell styles in the gallery	As you do, the cell you selected previews the cell styles.
5 Click as shown	
	To apply the Title style to the cell.
6 Select A6:H11	You'll apply a table style to the selection.
7 In the Styles group, click **Format As Table**	A gallery of built-in table styles appears, as shown in Exhibit 5-13.
Select the indicated table style	
	The Format As Table dialog box appears. Because you've already selected the range, it appears in the data location box.
Click **OK**	To apply the new style and close the dialog box. The Ribbon changes to display the Table Tools groups.
8 In the Table Styles group, click	(The More button is in the lower-right corner of the Table Styles group.) To display the gallery of table styles.
Move the pointer over the table styles in the gallery	As you do, the cells you selected preview the table styles.
Click anywhere in the worksheet	To close the Table Styles gallery.
Click any cell that's not in the table area	To close the Table Tools tab and return to the Home tab.

9	Observe the table	The table style has made some text bold, filled cells with color, resized columns to fit data, and applied borders. Each column label's cell has a list button. These buttons are for sorting, filtering, and hiding or showing data.
10	Click the down-arrow in the Total column, as shown	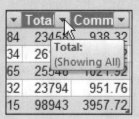
		To display the Sort and Show list.
	Choose **Sort Smallest to Largest**	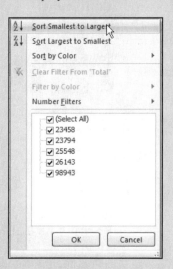
		To sort the data in the table and close the list.
11	Observe the table	All of the data is now sorted by the values in the Total column.
12	Click the down-arrow in the Name column	You'll hide some of the table data.
	Clear the check box beside **Audrey Kress**	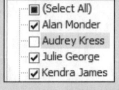
	Click **OK**	To hide the data in this row and close the list.
13	Observe the table	The row that includes the data for Audrey Kress has been hidden. The totals and commission calculations are unaffected.
	Show the hidden row	Click the down-arrow in the Name column, check the box for Audrey Kress, and click OK.

14	Sort the table by employee number	(Click the down-arrow in the Emp # column and choose Sort Smallest to Largest.) To return the table to its original sort order.
15	Update and close the workbook	

Finding and replacing formats

Explanation

You can use the Find and Replace dialog box to search for and replace formats. This is very useful in a large worksheet where you cannot see every cell on screen at once. To use Find and Replace to replace formatting:

1 Activate the Home tab (if necessary).

2 In the Editing group, click Find & Select, and then choose Replace to open the Find and Replace dialog box.

3 Click Options to expand the dialog box.

4 Beside Find what, click Format to open the Replace Format dialog box.

5 Click Format and select the cell or range whose formatting you want to replace.

6 Click the second Format button beside "Replace with" to open the Replace Format dialog box.

7 Click Choose Format From Cell, and select the cell whose formatting you want to copy.

8 Click Find Next.

9 Click Replace or Replace All.

10 Click Close.

Do it!

E-4:   Using Find and Replace to change cell formats

Here's how	Here's why
1 Open Product managers	(From the current unit folder.) You'll use Find and Replace to format all instances of a product manager's name in a large worksheet.
Save the workbook as **My product managers**	
2 In the Editing group, click **Find & Select**	To display the Find & Select menu.
Choose **Replace...**	To open the Find and Replace dialog box.
Click **Options**	To expand the dialog box.
3 In the Find What box, type **Melissa James**	To specify what to search for.
4 Click **Format** as shown	
	(The second Format button.) To open the Replace Format dialog box.
Activate the Font tab	
In the Font Style list, select **Bold Italic**	
Click **OK**	To select the format and close the dialog box.
5 In the Find and Replace dialog box, click **Replace All**	To make the replacements. A message box appears, indicating the number of replacements made.
Click **OK**	To close the message box.
6 Click **Close**	To close the Find and Replace dialog box.
7 Scroll down the worksheet	To see the rest of the data. All cells that contain Melissa James's name have been formatted in bold italics.
8 Update and close the workbook	

Unit summary: Formatting worksheets

Topic A　　In this topic, you learned how to format worksheets, including how to apply text formatting, such as **bold** and **italic**, and how to select a **font** and **font size**. You also learned how to select a **non-contiguous range**, and you saw that several text-formatting options are available on the Font tab in the **Format Cells dialog box**.

Topic B　　In this topic, you learned how to apply formatting to rows and columns and how to change column widths and row heights. You learned that you can use **alignment buttons** to set the alignment of data within a cell, or use the **Merge & Center button** to align data over a range.

Topic C　　In this topic, you learned how to format numbers. You learned that you can apply **currency** and **percentage** formats by using buttons in the Number group. You also learned how to change the number of decimal places displayed for a number. You viewed some of the number format categories in the **Format Cells dialog box**.

Topic D　　In this topic, you learned how to apply **conditional formats** based on criteria you specify. You learned how to create, edit, and delete conditional formatting.

Topic E　　In this topic, you learned how to copy formats by using the **Format Painter** and **AutoFill**. You learned that you can format a cell by using **cell styles**, and format an entire table by applying **table styles**. You also learned that you can use **Find and Replace** to change cell formats.

Independent practice activity

In this activity, you'll format data in a workbook by using a variety of methods.

1　Open Practice format and save it as **My practice format**.

2　Format A1 as Times New Roman, bold, 18 pt, and center it over the range A1:E1.

3　Format A2 as Times New Roman, italic, 12 pt, and center it over the range A2:E2.

4　Format the range A4:E4 as bold, and apply a heavy border below it.

5　Add a thin border below row 12.

6　Center the contents of the range B4:E4 within their cells.

7　Resize column A so that you can see all the names in the column.

8　Format the range D5:D12 as currency with zero decimal places.

9　Format the range E5:E12 as percentages with no decimal places.

10　Deselect the range and compare your work to Exhibit 5-14.

11　Apply a table style of your choice to the table data.

12　Update and close the workbook.

1	Outlander Spices				
2	*Employee information: Sales division*				
3					
4	**Name**	**Emp #**	**Region**	**Salary**	**Ret. plan**
5	Alan Monder	426587	Northern	$ 40,000	4%
6	Audrey Kress	422391	Northern	$ 38,000	2%
7	James Hanover	421424	Southern	$ 37,000	10%
8	Julie George	429192	Northern	$ 48,000	0%
9	Karen Anderson	426763	Southern	$ 44,000	6%
10	Kelly Palmatier	429669	Southern	$ 54,000	7%
11	Kendra James	426656	Northern	$ 37,000	12%
12	Michael Bobrow	424678	Southern	$ 52,000	0%

Exhibit 5-14: The workbook after Step 10 of the independent practice activity

Review questions

1 What is a non-contiguous range?

2 List three ways you can change the width of a column.

3 Where are the alignment buttons located?

4 What is conditional formatting?

5 What is a cell style?

Unit 6

Printing

Unit time: 45 minutes

Complete this unit, and you'll be able to:

A Preview how a worksheet will look when printed, use the spelling checker and the Research task pane, and use Find and Replace to change data.

B Control page orientation, set margins, create headers and footers, and hide or display gridlines and column and row headings.

C Print a worksheet, and work with print areas.

Topic A: Preparing to print

This topic covers the following Microsoft Certified Application Specialist exam objective for Excel 2007.

#	Objective
1.4.1	Change views within a single window
	• Change view to
	• normal
	• page break preview

Previewing a worksheet for errors

Explanation

Before printing a worksheet, you should preview it and check for spelling errors. Completing these tasks before you print can save time and paper.

Using the spelling checker

The spelling checker finds and corrects spelling errors. Check an entire worksheet by selecting a single cell, or check part of a worksheet by selecting a range of cells.

When you check an entire worksheet, the spelling checker examines such elements as cell contents, comments, graphics, and headers and footers. The search for errors begins at the cell you've selected, and the spelling checker prompts you to continue from the beginning when it reaches the end of the worksheet.

The spelling checker will suggest possible corrections if the word it finds is close to an entry in the program's dictionary. If the word isn't close, no suggestions will be offered. You can select the correct spelling from the suggestions if you find it there, or supply your own correction.

You can also choose to ignore a word that has been flagged by the spelling checker. For example, names are words that are typically not included in the spelling checker's dictionary. If the spelling checker flags a name or other word as a possible misspelling, you can add it to the dictionary on your PC's hard disk so that the word will be accepted the next time the spelling checker encounters it.

To check spelling in a worksheet or a range:

1 Select a cell if you want to check the entire worksheet, or select the specific range you want to check.

2 Activate the Review tab.

3 In the Proofing group, click Proofing Tools and choose Spelling. The Spelling dialog box appears.

4 For each word that isn't found in the dictionary, you can choose to change the spelling, ignore it, or add the word to the dictionary. If you choose to change the found word to one of the suggested spellings, you can do so for the current occurrence only or for all occurrences in the worksheet.

5 Continue through the worksheet or range by responding to each suggestion.

6 Click OK to close the message box when the spelling check is complete.

Do it!

A-1: Checking spelling in a worksheet

Here's how	Here's why
1 Open Spellcheck	(In the current unit folder.) You'll check this worksheet for spelling errors.
Verify that A1 is the active cell	
Save the workbook as **My spellcheck**	In the current unit folder.
2 Activate the Review tab	To display the tools on the Review tab.
3 In the Proofing group, click **Spelling**	To open the Spelling dialog box. The text "Quaterly" appears in the Not in Dictionary box. The correct spelling of the word "Quarterly" appears in the Suggestions box.
4 Click **Change**	To correct the misspelled word in the worksheet. "Burkhardt" appears in the Not in Dictionary box.
5 Click **Ignore All**	To prevent Mr. Burkhardt's name from being flagged as a misspelling in this worksheet. "Cardamon" appears in the Not in Dictionary box.
6 Observe the Suggestions box	Two suggestions for correcting the spelling appear. "Cardamom" is selected.
Click **Change**	To correct the word. The Spelling dialog box closes. A message box appears, indicating that the spelling check is complete for the entire sheet.
Click **OK**	To close the message box.

The Research task pane

Explanation

You can use the Research task pane to look up and insert definitions of and synonyms for words. To display definitions or synonyms in the Research pane, press Alt and click the cell containing the word you want to look up. In the list of reference books, choose the reference you want.

Do it!

A-2: Using the Research task pane

Here's how	Here's why
1 While pressing (ALT), select A4	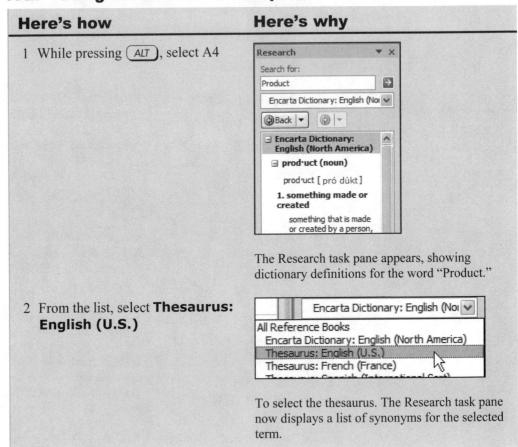
	The Research task pane appears, showing dictionary definitions for the word "Product."
2 From the list, select **Thesaurus: English (U.S.)**	
	To select the thesaurus. The Research task pane now displays a list of synonyms for the selected term.

3 In the Research pane, point to
   manufactured goods, as
   shown

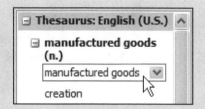

A border appears around the text, and a down-
arrow appears next to the text.

Click the down-arrow

To display a menu.

Choose **Insert**

4	Manufactured goods

To insert the text into A4.

4 Undo the action   To restore the original text in A4.

5 Close the Research pane   Click the X in the upper-right corner of the task
                                      pane.

6 Update the workbook

Finding and replacing values and text

Explanation

When you're replacing values or text, it can be difficult to scroll through the entire worksheet to find the specific value, especially when the worksheet is large. You can use the Find and Replace commands to search for one or more occurrences of a specific value and replace it with a new value.

The Replace command opens the Find and Replace dialog box, which can search rows, columns, or the entire worksheet for formulas, values, or text. After finding the specified value or text, this same dialog box can be used to replace it.

To search for and replace values or text:

1   Select the range you want to search. If you want to search the entire worksheet, click any cell.

2   In the Home tab's Editing group, click Find & Select.

3   Choose Replace to open the Find and Replace dialog box.

4   In the Find what box, enter the value or text you want to find.

5   Click Find Next. If you're finished, stop here.

6   In the Replace with box, enter the new value or text.

7   Click Replace to replace the highlighted result of the search and to search again. To replace all instances of the value or text, click Replace All.

Do it!

A-3: Finding and replacing text

Here's how	Here's why
1 Activate the Home tab	You'll replace all instances of one of the names in the Product Manager list.
2 In the Editing group, click **Find & Select**	To display the Find & Select menu.
Choose **Replace...**	To open the Find and Replace dialog box.
In the Find what box, type **Melissa James**	(If necessary.) To search for this name, which needs to be replaced.
Click **Find Next**	G5 becomes the active cell. It has a dark border around it, and the formula bar shows the text you entered as the search criteria.
3 In the Replace with box, type **Lee Jones**	To replace the text in G5 with the new text.
Click **Format**, as shown	

Melissa James ▾	No Format Set	Format... ▾
Lee Jones ▾	*Preview*	Format.... ▾

	To open the Replace Format dialog box.
4 Activate the Font tab	If necessary.
From the Font Style list, select **Italic**	To replace not only the text but the text style.
Click **OK**	To close the dialog box.
5 In the Find and Replace dialog box, click **Replace**	Excel replaces the text in G5 with "Lee Jones" and moves to the next instance of that text, in G6.
6 Click **Replace All**	To replace all instances of "Melissa James" with "Lee Jones." A message box informs you that Excel has completed its search and made three replacements.
Click **OK**	To close the message box.
7 Click **Close**	To close the Find and Replace dialog box.
Update and close the workbook	

Print Preview

Explanation

The Print Preview command shows you what a worksheet will look like when printed. Previewing worksheets can save paper and show you how page setup choices will affect a printout. Click the Office Button and choose Print, Print Preview to preview a worksheet. Exhibit 6-1 shows the Print Preview window.

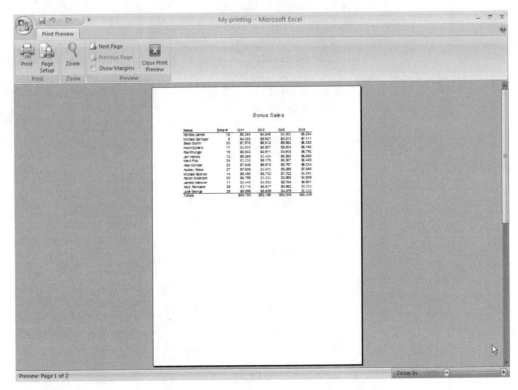

Exhibit 6-1: The Print Preview window

When you point to the previewed worksheet, the pointer takes the shape of a magnifying glass. You can then click to zoom in on the preview. The following table describes the buttons on the Print Preview tab:

Button	Used to...
Next Page	Display the next page to be printed.
Previous Page	Display the previous page to be printed.
Zoom	Switch between magnified and full-page views of the worksheet.
Print	Set the printing options and print the worksheet.
Page Setup	Set the options for controlling the appearance of the printed sheets.
Show Margins	Display the margin handles, which you can move to adjust the margins.
Close Print Preview	Close the Print Preview window.

Page Layout view

The Page Layout View button on the status bar displays the worksheet in layout view. You can zoom out to show all pages in the worksheet, as shown in Exhibit 6-2.

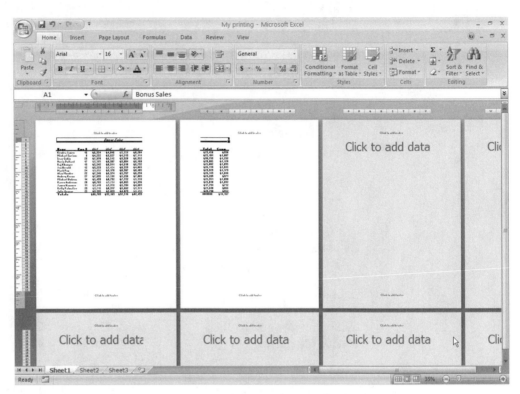

Exhibit 6-2: Page Layout view, zoomed out to show multiple pages

A-4:   Previewing a worksheet

Here's how	Here's why
1 Open **Printing**	This workbook contains sales information for Outlander Spices' sales representatives.
2 Save the workbook as **My printing**	In the current unit folder.
3 Click	
Choose **Print**, **Print Preview**	To open the Print Preview window for the worksheet, as shown in Exhibit 6-1
4 Point to the preview	The pointer takes the shape of a magnifying glass.
Click the preview	To zoom in on it. You can use the scrollbars to view different parts of the worksheet.
Click the preview again	To zoom out.
5 In the Preview group, click **Show Margins**	To display margin lines on the preview. You can adjust the margins by dragging the black boxes at the ends of the margin lines.
Click **Show Margins** again	To turn off the display of margin lines.
6 Press (PAGE DOWN)	To display the next page. The data is too wide to fit on a single page, so the last column prints by itself on a separate page. You'll fix this in an upcoming activity.
7 In the Preview group, click **Close Print Preview**	To close the Print Preview window.
8 Click	(The Page Layout View button is on the status bar.) To view the sheet in Page Layout mode.
9 Zoom out to better show multiple pages	(Drag the Zoom slider on the status bar to the left.) This view of the worksheet shows all of the populated pages, plus blank pages for unpopulated areas, as shown in Exhibit 6-2.
Zoom in to approximately 85% zoom level	Drag the slider on the status bar.
Click	(The Normal View button is on the status bar.) To return to Normal view. This view was set to 100% zoom.

Topic B: Page Setup options

This topic covers the following Microsoft Certified Application Specialist exam objectives for Excel 2007.

#	Objective
2.1.2	**Show and hide gridlines and headers** • Hide gridlines for presentation purposes • Hide headers for presentation purposes
5.5.3	**Set margins** • Set worksheet margins to specified values
5.5.4	**Add and modify headers and footers** • Change the date or other information in a footer
5.5.5	**Change the orientation of a worksheet**
5.5.6	**Scale worksheet content to fit a printed page**

The Page Layout tab

Explanation

The Page Layout tab contains options to help you control various aspects of a worksheet's printed appearance.

Orientation and Scale to Fit

Use the Orientation gallery in the Page Setup group on the Page Layout tab to change the orientation of a worksheet. For worksheets that take up more than a page, the options in the Scale to Fit group can be useful. The data in the worksheet can be condensed to fit within the number of pages you specify.

B-1:   Setting page orientation

Here's how	Here's why
1 Activate the Page Layout tab	You'll set page orientation and scaling.
2 In the Page Setup group, click **Orientation** and choose **Landscape**	To specify a landscape, or wide, orientation for the printout.
Preview the page	(Click the Office Button and choose Print, Print Preview, or click the Page Layout View button on the status bar.) To see how the worksheet will look when printed in landscape orientation.
Close the preview	Click Close Print Preview.
3 Click **Orientation** and choose **Portrait**	(In the Page Setup group.) To return to a Portrait orientation.
4 Observe the Scale to Fit group	
	You can adjust the scaling of the printout. When you have more data than will fit on a page, you can use the Width and Height lists to resize the worksheet to fit within a specific number of pages.
In the Width box, select **1 page**	To scale the worksheet so that it fits on a single sheet of paper.
5 Preview the page	(Use Print Preview.) The data now fits on a single page. Scaling to fit reduced the size of the text, which may make it difficult to read.
Return to the worksheet	
6 In the Width box, choose **Automatic**	You'll use a different method to place all of the data on one page.
Change the value in the Scale box to 100%	To return the scaling to normal.

Margins

Explanation

You have already seen that you can adjust margins in the Print Preview window. The Margins gallery in the Page Setup group offers some standard margin settings. To create custom margin settings, click Advanced in the Margins gallery. This displays the Margins tab of the Page Setup dialog box, shown in Exhibit 6-3. You can use the "Center on page" options to center the data either horizontally or vertically; this centering can make your worksheets look more organized.

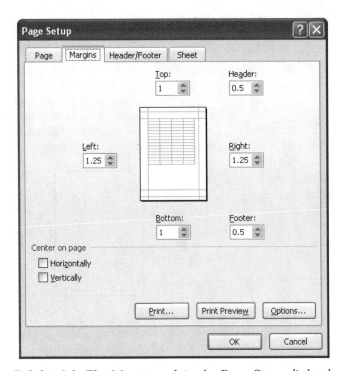

Exhibit 6-3: The Margins tab in the Page Setup dialog box

B-2:   Setting margins

Here's how	Here's why
1 In the Scale to Fit group, verify that Width and Height are set to Automatic, and that the Scale is 100%	
2 In the Page Setup group, click **Margins**	To display the Margins gallery. Several standard margin setups are listed.
Choose **Custom Margins...**	To open the Page Setup dialog box. The Margins tab, shown in Exhibit 6-3, is displayed by default. You can set the left, right, top, bottom, header, and footer margins to specific values (they are measured in inches). You can also center the data on the page.
3 Under Center on page, check **Vertically**	
	To specify that you want to center the data vertically on the page. The preview shows how the data will look.
Clear **Vertically**	To move the data back to the top of the page.
4 Check **Horizontally**	To center the data horizontally on the page. Many worksheets look better centered horizontally.
5 In the Left box, click the down-arrow three times to select **0.5**	To change the left margin from one and one-quarter inches to half an inch.
Set the right margin to **0.5**	In the Right box, click the down-arrow.
6 Click **Print Preview**	To preview the worksheet. The data now fits on a single page, and the text size is not reduced.
Close Print Preview	To close the preview, save the margin settings, and return to the worksheet.
7 Update the workbook	

Headers and footers

Explanation

A header and footer on each page help the reader identify the printed information, such as the current date, page number, author, workbook or worksheet name, and company name, as well as various combinations of these options.

To add a header or footer:

1   Activate the Insert tab.

2   In the Text group, click Header & Footer. The workbook changes to Page Layout View, and the Headers & Footers tab is activated. A header box opens in the top center of the first page.

3   Add your text and any other elements, such as the date, that you want to include.

You can add items from the Header & Footer Elements group in the Header & Footer Tools tab. The group is shown in Exhibit 6-4.

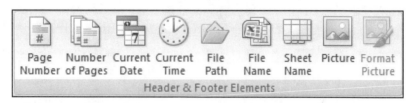

Exhibit 6-4: The Header & Footer Elements group on the Header & Footer Tools tab

Text and elements can be placed in a header or footer's left, center, and right sections, as shown in Exhibit 6-5. You can move between sections by pressing Tab to move to the right or Shift+Tab to move to the left.

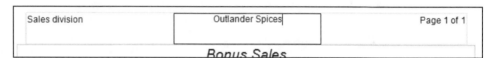

Exhibit 6-5: Header elements in the left, center, and right sections

To format text and other elements in the header and footer, you can use the Font group and other formatting tools on the Home tab.

B-3:   Creating and editing headers and footers

Here's how	Here's why
1 Activate the Insert tab	
2 In the Text group, click **Header & Footer**	The worksheet switches to Page Layout View, the Header & Footer Tools tab appears, and the insertion point moves to a header box in the center of the first page.
3 Type **Outlander Spices**	To add header text that is centered on the page.
4 Press (SHIFT) + (TAB)	To move to the left header box.
Type **Sales division**	To add header text that is aligned with the left side of the page.
5 Press (TAB) twice	To move to the right header box. You'll add a header that combines text and predefined elements.
6 Type **Page**	To begin a page numbering element.
Type a space	To place a space between the word and the element that will follow it.
In the Header and Footer Elements group, click **Page Number**	To insert an element that prints the current page number.
7 Type a space	
Type **of**	
Type a space	
Click **Number of Pages**	(In the Header & Footer Elements group.) To insert an element that prints the total number of pages in the workbook.
8 Click any cell on the first page of the workbook	To deselect the header.
Observe the header	The right-side element reads "Page 1 of 1."
9 Scroll to the bottom of the page	You'll add a footer.
Click the right side of the footer section	To select the section and make it editable.
Type today's date	Use the mm/dd/yyyy format.
Deselect the footer	Instead of a static date, you need to enter a date function that will show the current date when the file is opened.

10	Click the right side of the footer section	To put the footer in edit mode.
	Delete the date you just typed	
11	In the Header and Footer Elements group, click **Current Date**	To insert an element that prints the current date on every page.
	Click an empty cell in the worksheet	To deselect the footer section.
12	Preview the worksheet	Use Print Preview.
13	Zoom in on the header and footer	Point to what you want to see, and click.
	Zoom out of the page	
14	Close the preview	
	Return to Normal view	Click the Normal icon in the status bar.
	Update the workbook	

Sheet options

Explanation

The Page Layout tab contains buttons and galleries that control preview and printing options. For example, you can print or suppress row and column headings or worksheet gridlines.

The Sheet tab of the Page Setup dialog box (shown in Exhibit 6-6) is useful for multi-page worksheets. You can use the Print titles section to define rows or columns that should be repeated on every page of the printout. You can specify the order in which Excel prints sections of the worksheet, and select other print options for the current worksheet.

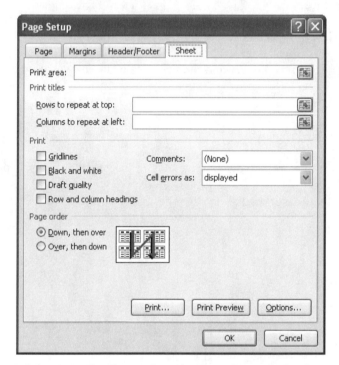

Exhibit 6-6: The Sheet tab in the Page Setup dialog box

Gridlines and column/row headings

There may be times when you'll want to see just the data on a worksheet, and not the gridlines or column and row headings. To hide these elements, activate the Page Layout tab on the Ribbon. In the Sheet Options group, under both Gridlines and Headings, clear the check boxes next to View.

Do it!   **B-4:   Hiding gridlines and headings**

Here's how	Here's why
1 Open Large worksheet	In the current unit folder.
Save the workbook as **My large worksheet**	
Activate the Page Layout tab	
2 In the Sheet Options group, under Gridlines, clear **View**	To hide the gridlines on the worksheet.
Hide the column and row headings	In the Sheet Options group, under Headings, clear View.
3 In the Sheet Options group, click [icon]	(The Dialog Box Launcher is in the bottom-right corner of the group.) To open the Page Setup dialog box.
4 Activate the Sheet tab	If necessary.
Observe the Print section	Print quality and other options appear here. You can choose to print gridlines or column and row headings.
5 Observe the Page order section	You can specify the order in which worksheet areas are divided into printable pages.
6 Preview the worksheet	Click Print Preview in the dialog box.
Close the preview	
Update and close the workbook	

Topic C: Printing worksheets

This topic covers the following Microsoft Certified Application Specialist exam objective for Excel 2007.

#	Objective
5.5.1	**Define the area of a worksheet to be printed**
	• Set a print area on a single sheet.

Printing

Explanation

Although there are several ways to provide output from Excel, the most common output is a printed worksheet. After you've set up a worksheet properly and previewed it, it's easy to print it.

The Print dialog box

When you click the Office Button and choose Print, the Print dialog box appears, as shown in Exhibit 6-7. Select the printer you want to use (if your computer is connected to more than one), specify a range of pages to print, specify the number of copies, and specify whether to print a selection, an active worksheet, or the entire workbook. You can also access a preview of the workbook from this dialog box.

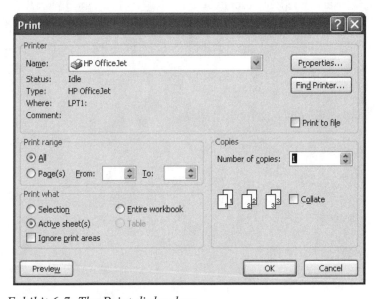

Exhibit 6-7: The Print dialog box

Printing a selection

When you don't want to clear a print area but you want to print a range within the defined print area, you can print a selection. To print a selection:

1 Select the range you want to print.
2 Click the Office Button and choose Print to open the Print dialog box.
3 Under Print what, click Selection.
4 Choose any other options you want to use in the dialog box.
5 Click OK.

Quick Print

You can print a worksheet without going through the Print dialog box. When you do so, Excel prints the active worksheet to the current printer by using the default settings. Click the Office Button and choose Print, Quick Print.

Do it!

C-1: Printing a worksheet

Here's how	Here's why
1 In My printing, select A1:H5	You'll print a selection from this worksheet.
2 Click [icon] and choose **Print**	To open the Print dialog box. It should resemble Exhibit 6-7. If you have multiple-page worksheets, you can use the Print range options to print only a specific page range.
Under Print what, click **Selection**	To specify that you want to print only the range selected in the worksheet.
3 Click **Preview**	To see that the printed page would include only the selected area of the worksheet.
Close the preview	
4 Deselect the range	To clear the selection.
5 Click [icon]	You'll print without using the Print dialog box.
Point as shown	[image of Print button with arrow]
	To display the Print list.
Choose **Quick Print**	To print the worksheet with all current settings.
6 Update the workbook	

Defining and clearing the print area

Explanation At times you might want to print only part of a worksheet. You can do this by defining a *print area*. Then only that part of the worksheet will print until you clear the print area or define a new one.

To define a print area, you select the range you want to print. Then, on the Page Layout tab, click Print Area and select Set Print Area. When you save a file, the print area is saved as well.

To clear the print area, click Print Area and select Clear Print Area from the list. Print areas can include non-contiguous ranges.

Do it! ### C-2: Working with the print area

Here's how	Here's why
1 Select A1:H8	You'll define a portion of the worksheet as the print area. You can also select non-contiguous ranges to print.
Activate the Page Layout tab	If necessary.
In the Page Setup group, click **Print Area** and choose **Set Print Area**	To set the print area.
2 In the Page Setup group, click **Print Titles**	To display the Sheet tab in the Page Setup dialog box. The range you specified appears in the Print Area box.
3 Preview the page	The preview shows only the cells that were defined as the print area.
Close the preview	
4 Click **Print Area** and choose **Clear Print Area**	To clear the print area you defined.
5 Update and close the workbook	

Unit summary: Printing

Topic A   In this topic, you learned how to check for misspelled words by using the **spelling checker**. You also learned how to use the **Research task pane** to find definitions and synonyms for a word. Next, you learned how to use the **Find** and **Replace** commands to find and change text or values. You learned how to **print** a worksheet and control its appearance. You also used the **Print Preview** command to preview a printout on screen. You also learned how to **zoom** in and out of the preview and how to view **margins** in the Preview window.

Topic B   In this topic, you learned how to use controls on the **Page Layout** tab and in the **Page Setup** dialog box. You learned how to change the **orientation** of the page and how to **center** a printout vertically or horizontally. You also learned how to set margins. Then, you learned how to create custom **headers** and **footers** and how to hide gridlines and headings.

Topic C   In this topic, you learned how to print a worksheet. You saw that you can use the **Print dialog box** to specify a **print range** and the number of copies. You learned how to print a worksheet in a single step by using the **Quick Print** option. You also learned how to set and clear a **print area**.

Independent practice activity

In this activity, you'll preview a worksheet, change the page orientation, scale the worksheet to fit on a page, create custom headers and footers, set the print area, and center the sheet on the page.

1 Open Practice printing and save it as **My practice printing**.

2 Preview the worksheet. The data appears on two pages.

3 Return to Normal view and change the orientation of the printout to Landscape.

4 Scale the printout to fit to 1 page wide by 1 page tall.

5 Create a custom header. In the left section, enter **Outlander Spices**. In the right section, enter **Sales division**.

6 Create a custom footer. In the left section, enter **Monthly sales figures**. In the right section, insert the current date.

7 Preview the worksheet, and compare the preview to Exhibit 6-8.

8 Close the preview.

9 Set A3:H18 as the print area.

10 Center the sheet horizontally. (*Hint:* Use the Margins tab in the Page Setup dialog box.)

11 Preview the worksheet, and compare the preview to Exhibit 6-9.

12 Close the preview.

13 Update and close the workbook.

Outlander Spices   Sales division

Bonus Sales

Name	Emp #	Jan	Feb	Mar	Apr	May	Jun	Jul	Aug	Sep	Oct	Nov	Dec	Total	Comm
Kendra James	16	6354	7975	3227	8296	7995	9529	7576	7765	7063	4846	3958	8284	$ 82,884	$ 3,315
Michael Springer	8	4222	3635	3806	9902	9838	8057	8599	4607	7405	9627	4213	7111	$ 81,030	$ 3,241
Sean Guhin	23	7978	3380	9345	4368	6040	3521	6867	5597	7350	6512	9928	6352	$ 77,261	$ 3,090
Norin Dollard	17	3909	3638	9565	5563	7164	3237	3850	5815	6841	8907	9004	6168	$ 73,678	$ 2,947
Raj Khunger	19	5542	9765	8888	6470	7390	6975	8941	8179	4367	8911	4618	6792	$ 86,857	$ 3,474
Jen Herold	12	9259	5222	7283	3530	9393	4243	3932	8854	8367	3424	8553	4865	$ 76,937	$ 3,077
Mark Pop	24	3335	4443	4590	3824	5662	8208	8285	6069	4704	9178	8307	8485	$ 75,114	$ 3,005
Alan Monder	22	7546	5145	3447	5228	8272	9197	8960	6747	3439	6574	5767	6234	$ 76,578	$ 3,063
Audrey Kress	27	7635	7257	9750	4702	7440	7411	6757	4728	9868	3500	5256	7865	$ 82,196	$ 3,288
Michael Bobrow	14	5493	4813	5079	8254	8652	6214	9393	4035	5149	8732	7722	3990	$ 77,540	$ 3,102
Karen Anderson	20	8765	8248	4309	3360	7233	5841	9036	7442	3683	3224	8865	4936	$ 74,962	$ 2,998
James Hanover	11	3440	5087	3737	9872	3955	7737	5589	3875	9730	3958	5784	4601	$ 67,376	$ 2,695
Kelly Palmatier	29	3716	8753	5872	7883	7756	5137	5066	9698	4421	8917	5662	3324	$ 76,234	$ 3,049
Julie George	25	9595	9770	9554	8290	8944	9470	5490	7977	4426	5859	4879	3432	$ 87,711	$ 3,508
Totals		86789	87131	88452	89542	105734	94777	98341	91388	86813	92169	92516	82439	$ 1,096,358	$ 43,854

Monthly sales figures   3/2/2006

Exhibit 6-8: The print preview of the worksheet after Step 7 of the independent practice activity

Outlander Spices   Sales division

Name	Emp #	Jan	Feb	Mar	Apr	May	Jun
Kendra James	16	6354	7975	3227	8296	7995	9529
Michael Springer	8	4222	3635	3806	9902	9838	8057
Sean Guhin	23	7978	3380	9345	4368	6040	3521
Norin Dollard	17	3909	3638	9565	5563	7164	3237
Raj Khunger	19	5542	9765	8888	6470	7390	6975
Jen Herold	12	9259	5222	7283	3530	9393	4243
Mark Pop	24	3335	4443	4590	3824	5662	8208
Alan Monder	22	7546	5145	3447	5228	8272	9197
Audrey Kress	27	7635	7257	9750	4702	7440	7411
Michael Bobrow	14	5493	4813	5079	8254	8652	6214
Karen Anderson	20	8765	8248	4309	3360	7233	5841
James Hanover	11	3440	5087	3737	9872	3955	7737
Kelly Palmatier	29	3716	8753	5872	7883	7756	5137
Julie George	25	9595	9770	9554	8290	8944	9470
Totals		86789	87131	88452	89542	105734	94777

Exhibit 6-9: The print preview of the worksheet after Step 11 of the independent practice activity

Review questions

1   If you wanted to find synonyms for a word, which task pane would you use?

2   How do you change the orientation of a worksheet for printing?

3   What is a print area?

4   How do you define a print area?

5   A print area must be a single range of contiguous cells. True or false?

Unit 7

Creating charts

Unit time: 35 minutes

Complete this unit, and you'll know how to:

A Create charts based on worksheet data, and move charts within a workbook.

B Change chart types, format chart elements, and move and resize embedded charts.

C Print chart sheets and embedded charts.

Topic A: Chart basics

This topic covers the following Microsoft Certified Applications Specialist exam objectives for Excel 2007.

#	Objective
4.1.1	**Select appropriate data sources for charts**
	• Select the appropriate data to create a column chart
4.1.2	**Select appropriate chart types to represent data sources**
	• Create a chart that shows what part of the budget the *x* department uses
4.2.1	**Add and remove chart elements**
	• Titles
4.2.2	**Move and size charts**
	• Move an embedded chart to a new sheet
	• Move an embedded chart from a chart sheet to a worksheet by embedding as an object
	• Size a chart while maintaining scale

Using charts in Excel

Explanation

Charts are graphic representations of data. A chart can communicate information much more effectively than a table full of numbers can. For example, it takes time to notice a trend in a table of data, but a sloping graph in a chart communicates the trend instantly.

Creating and moving charts

A chart can be created based on data contained in a worksheet. A chart can be an object embedded within a worksheet or placed on a separate chart sheet in a workbook. Charts are easy to create and customize by using the controls on the Ribbon.

To create a chart:

1   Select the data that you want to include in the chart. The data should include all the values you want to display in the chart and any text that identifies those values.

2   On the Ribbon, activate the Insert tab.

3   In the Charts group, click the desired chart type; then choose a sub-type from the gallery to insert the chart in the worksheet.

4   While the chart is selected, Excel 2007 displays the Chart Tools set of contextual tabs: Design, Layout, and Format. Use the options in these tabs to format and customize the chart. Some options include using Quick Styles and Quick Layouts to quickly format your chart.

To move a chart within a worksheet, first select it. Point to the border of the chart and drag to the location you want. To resize an embedded chart, you select it, point to one of the sizing handles in the border, and then drag it.

Do it!

A-1: Creating a chart

Here's how	Here's why
1 Open Charts	(From the current unit folder.) This workbook contains some simple data from which you'll create some charts.
Save the workbook as **My charts**	In the current unit folder.
2 Select A3:E7	This is the range for which you'll create a chart.
3 Activate the Insert tab	If necessary.
In the Charts group, click **Column**	To display the Column gallery.
4 Observe the column types	There are 2-D and 3-D types, as well as Cylinder, Cone, and Pyramid types.
In the Charts group, click **Line**	To display the Line gallery, which displays thumbnail images of the different line charts available.
Move the pointer over the thumbnails gallery	To see the Enhanced ScreenTip that appears for each line chart.
5 Click **Column**	To begin a column chart.
Click the indicated thumbnail	
	To insert a 3-D Clustered Column chart.
6 Observe the Ribbon	The Ribbon displays the Chart Tools contextual tabs: Design, Layout, and Format.
7 Activate the Layout tab	The Layout tab provides selections for customizing your chart.
In the Labels group, click **Chart Title**	To display the gallery of chart titles.

8 Choose **Above Chart**	To place a centered title above the chart.
Edit the chart title text to read **Outlander Spices**	
Click anywhere on the chart	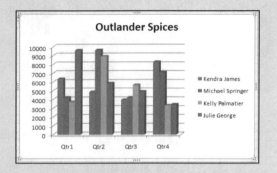
	To deselect the title.
9 Point to the border around the chart	The pointer changes to a four-headed arrow.
Drag the chart down and to the right	(If necessary.) To move the chart so that you can see the data in A3:E7.
10 Edit B7 to read **500**	To change the value of one of the chart elements.
Observe the chart	Changing the data changed the chart. The column that was the tallest is now the shortest.
Click ↰	To undo the editing and return cell B7 to its original value. The chart reflects the change.
Update the workbook	

Moving charts within workbooks

Explanation

In addition to moving a chart within a worksheet, you can move a chart to a separate sheet, known as a chart sheet. A chart sheet shows only the chart, not the data from which it was drawn.

To move a chart to a chart sheet:

1 Select the chart to activate the Chart Tools contextual tabs.
2 Activate the Design tab.
3 In the Location group, click Move Chart to open the Move Chart dialog box.
4 Under "Choose where you want the chart to be placed," select New sheet, and enter a name for the chart sheet.
5 Click OK.

When a chart is placed in a worksheet containing the data it represents, it is placed as an *embedded object.* You can place a chart-sheet chart as an embedded object within a worksheet. To do so, open the Move Chart dialog box, select Object in, and select the worksheet in which you want to place the chart.

Do it!

A-2: Moving a chart within a workbook

Here's how	Here's why
1 Select the chart	To activate the Chart Tools.
Activate the Design tab	You'll move the chart to a new sheet.
2 In the Location group, click **Move Chart**	To open the Move Chart dialog box.
Select **New sheet**	To create a chart sheet.
In the box, type **Bonus Chart**	⊙ New sheet: Bonus Chart
	To name the new chart sheet.
Click **OK**	To close the dialog box and switch to the new chart sheet.
3 Adjust the zoom so that the chart fits in the window	(If necessary.) Click the Zoom percentage on the status bar, choose Fit selection from the Zoom dialog box, and click OK.
4 Observe the worksheet tabs in the status bar	A new sheet tab named Bonus Chart appears before the default sheets.
5 Select the chart	If necessary.
Open the Move Chart dialog box	In the Location group, click Move Chart.
Under "Choose where you want the chart to be placed," select **Object in**	
Verify that Sheet1 appears in the list, and click **OK**	To close the dialog box and place the chart as an object in Sheet1. The Bonus Chart sheet disappears.
6 Move the chart to a chart sheet	Open the Move Chart dialog box and select New sheet. Name the sheet "Bonus Chart" and click OK.
7 Update the workbook	

Chart terminology

Explanation

Terms that describe individual chart elements are listed in the table below and shown in Exhibit 7-1.

Chart element	Description
Value axis	Provides the scale for all data points in the chart, based on the values in the selected range.
Category axis	Includes the labels for all categories in the chart, as defined in the first row of data in the selected range.
Data point	The value from one cell in the selected range.
Data series	The values from all cells in a category.
Legend	Identifies the data series in the chart.

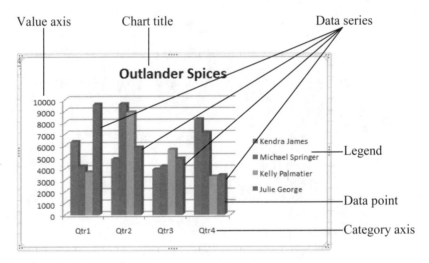

Exhibit 7-1: Chart elements

Do it!

A-3:   Examining chart elements

Here's how	**Here's why**
1 Point to the first column in Qtr1	A ScreenTip appears. This data point is from the series of data points for Kendra James. The data point is for Qtr1. The value of this data point is 6,354. In this chart, each column represents a data point.
2 Point to the first column for each quarter	These four columns make up a series. Each series in this chart represents the sales figures for a specific sales rep. This series represents Kendra James's sales in all four quarters.
3 Observe the legend	■ Kendra James ■ Michael Springer ■ Kelly Palmatier ■ Julie George This chart's legend comes from the first column of the data you selected for the series.
4 Observe the four Qtr1 columns	Qtr1 is a category. Each category contains a data point from each series.
5 Observe the category axis	As shown in Exhibit 7-1. Text for categories in this chart comes from the first row of data you selected for the series.
6 Observe the value axis	As shown in Exhibit 7-1. The scale for the value axis is generated automatically based on the minimum and maximum data points in the selected range.

Working with embedded charts

Explanation

Embedded charts are useful because they allow you to see your worksheet data and your chart on the same sheet. This can be handy when you want to print a report.

Dynamic charts

There is a link between the data from which you create a chart and the chart itself. Therefore, if you update any of the source data, the change will be reflected immediately in any charts based on that data.

Do it!

A-4:   Using an embedded chart

Here's how	Here's why
1 Activate the **Sheet2** worksheet	You'll create a pie chart showing the percentage of the budget for each department.
2 Select A4:A9	This range will supply the text for the legend in the chart.
While holding ⸨CTRL⸩, select C4:C9	<table><tr><td>**Department**</td><td>**% Yearly budget**</td></tr><tr><td>Marketing</td><td>23%</td></tr><tr><td>Sales</td><td>25%</td></tr><tr><td>Human Resources</td><td>12%</td></tr><tr><td>Customer Support</td><td>10%</td></tr><tr><td>Other</td><td>30%</td></tr></table>
	To add the %Yearly budget column to the selection. This column will provide the data for the chart. The selection should look similar to the picture shown here.
3 Open the Pie chart gallery	On the Insert tab, in the Charts group, click Pie.
From the thumbnails, select the indicated chart	
	To create a 3-D pie chart. The Chart Tools tab appears.

4   Activate the Format tab

In the Size group, click as shown

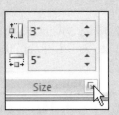

To open the Size and Properties dialog box. You'll resize the chart to make it smaller.

Verify that the Size tab is activated

5   Under Scale, edit both the Height and Width values to **75%**

To decrease the chart's size by 25%.

Check **Lock aspect ratio**

To maintain the same ratio between the height and width after resizing.

Click **Close**

To close the dialog box and apply the new size.

6   Drag the chart to the area below the data

(Point to the chart border and drag.) Make sure you can see both the table and its chart.

7   Edit C5 to read **50%**

To change the Marketing budget data and see the result in the pie chart.

Observe the change in the chart

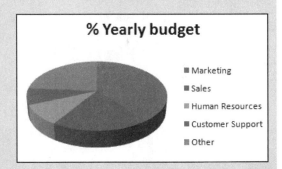

The Marketing section is now considerably larger. The chart is dynamically linked to the worksheet data.

8   Undo the change

To revert to the original value in C5.

9   Update the workbook

Topic B: Modifying charts

This topic covers the following Microsoft Certified Applications Specialist exam objectives for Excel 2007.

#	Objective
4.1.3	**Format charts using Quick Styles** • Quick Styles • Quick Layouts
4.2.1	**Add and remove chart elements** • Axis information • Legends
4.2.3	**Change chart types**

Chart options

Explanation

You can modify charts by changing the chart type, applying various Quick Styles and Quick Layouts, by adding various labels, and moving or resizing the entire chart or just a part of it.

Chart types

To change the chart type, select the chart and then click Change Chart Type in the Type group on the Design tab. (This Design tab is one of the Chart Tools contextual tabs.) The Change Chart Type gallery opens. Select a chart type and sub-type, and click OK.

Do it!

B-1: Changing a chart type

Here's how	Here's why
1 Activate the **Bonus Chart** worksheet	
Click the chart	To select it. The Chart Tools contextual tabs appear on the Ribbon.
2 Activate the Design tab	You'll choose another type for this chart.
In the Type group, click **Change Chart Type**	To open the Change Chart Type dialog box.
3 From the Chart Type list, select **Bar**	Bar charts resemble column charts lying on their sides.
From the thumbnails list, select the indicated type	
	To change the chart to a Clustered Horizontal Cylinder type.
Click **OK**	To close the dialog box and apply the change.
4 Try several chart types	Use the Change Chart Type dialog box to select different combinations.
5 Return the chart type to 3-D Clustered Column	

Quick Styles and Quick Layouts

Explanation

Excel provides predefined styles and layouts you can use to format your charts quickly and easily. To use Quick Styles and Quick Layouts, select the chart and activate the Design contextual tab. In the Chart Layouts and Chart Styles groups, pick the layout or style you want to apply to your chart. An example is shown in Exhibit 7-2.

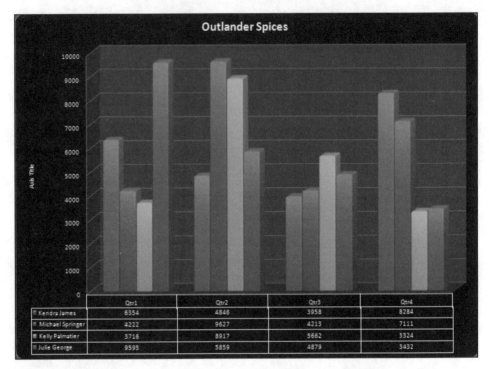

Exhibit 7-2: The Bonus Chart with a predefined layout and style applied

Do it!

B-2: Applying Quick Layouts and Quick Styles

Here's how	Here's why
1 Verify that the chart is selected	You'll experiment with applying different layouts and styles to the chart.
2 Activate the Design tab	If necessary.

3 In the Chart Layout group, click as shown

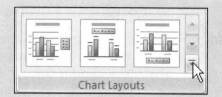

To open the Quick Layout gallery.

Select the indicated chart layout

To apply Layout 5 to the chart.

Observe the chart

The staff names have been placed in the bottom-left area of the chart, and the sales data from the worksheet appears below the chart.

4 In the Chart Styles group, click as shown

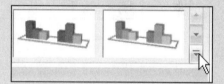

To open the Chart Quick Styles gallery.

Select the indicated style

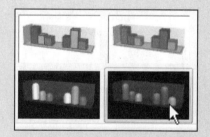

To apply Style 42 to the chart. Your chart should look like that shown in Exhibit 7-2.

5 Apply Layout 1 to the chart

In the Chart Layouts group, click Layout 1.

6 Apply Style 2 to the chart

In the Chart Styles group, click Style 2. The chart appears as it did at the beginning of the activity.

Update the workbook

Formatting chart objects

The various parts of a chart are called *objects*. For some objects, you have several formatting choices, such as position, font, and font size. For other objects, you can control only the color of the fill and the line around it. To format a chart object, right-click it and choose a format option.

Alternatively, you can select chart elements from the drop-down list in the Current Selection group on the Ribbon's Format tab (one of the Chart Tools contextual tabs). You can then format the selection by using options in the Shape Styles, WordArt Styles, Arrange, and Size groups on the Ribbon.

Adding a title and axis labels

To add a title or axis label to your chart:

1 Select the chart.

2 Activate the Layout tab.

3 In the Labels group, click Axis Titles.

4 Choose a horizontal or vertical axis title.

B-3: Formatting chart elements

Here's how	Here's why
1 Activate the Format tab	You'll format some of the objects on this chart.
In the Current Selection group, from the drop-down list, select **Series "Kendra James"**	To select the four data points in this series.
2 In the Shape Styles group, click as shown	
	To display the Shape Fill gallery.
3 Under Theme Colors, click **Orange, Accent 6** as shown	
	To give the columns for this data series an orange color.
4 Give Kelly Palmatier's data series an aqua accent color	In the Current Selection group, select Series "Kelly Palmatier" from the list. Then, in the Shape Styles group, display the Shape Fill gallery. Under Theme Colors, click Aqua, Accent 5.
Give Julie George's data series a dark blue accent color	Choose Dark Blue, Text 2.

5   Select **Series "Michael Springer"**

From the list in the Current Selection group.

Click the column for the Qtr2 data point

To select just that data point in the data series.

Right-click the Qtr2 data point and choose **Add Data Label** from the shortcut menu

To display the value of the data point at the top of the column.

Deselect the column and observe the chart

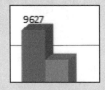

The value now appears above the column for that data point.

6   Activate the Layout tab

You'll label the vertical axis.

In the Labels group, click **Axis Titles** and choose **Primary Vertical Axis Title**, **Rotated Title**

To insert a rotated title along the vertical axis. The label "Axis Title" appears.

7   Click within the Axis Title box

To make the text editable.

Edit the text to read **Bonus Sales in Dollars**

8   Update the workbook

Modifying embedded charts

Explanation

The Layout tab—available when you select a chart—contains a Labels group. Use the options in the Labels group to modify the chart title, legend, and data labels. Exhibit 7-3 shows a chart with a legend displayed below it instead of on the side.

Exhibit 7-3: The embedded chart in the My charts workbook

Do it!

B-4:   Modifying an embedded chart

Here's how	Here's why
1 Activate Sheet2	
2 Select the embedded chart	(Click anywhere in the chart's white space.) Sizing handles appear around the chart. If you click a specific chart element, you'll select that element instead of the entire chart.
Move the chart under the worksheet data	If necessary.
3 Activate the Layout tab	(If necessary.) You'll hide, show, and then move the legend.
In the Labels group, click **Legend** and choose **None**	To hide the legend.
4 In the Labels group, click **Legend**	To display the Legend menu. The chart is more useful with the legend showing.
Choose **Show Legend at Bottom**	To move the legend to beneath the pie chart.
5 Select the chart again	If necessary.
Drag one of the middle-right sizing handles to the right edge of column E	To make the chart slightly smaller.
6 Deselect the chart	Compare your worksheet to Exhibit 7-3.
7 Update the workbook	

Topic C: Printing charts

Explanation

You print charts the same way you print worksheets.

Page Setup options

For an embedded chart, the Page Setup options are exactly the same as those for the worksheet in which they reside. For chart sheets, the Page Setup dialog box has a Chart tab (instead of a Sheet tab), as shown in Exhibit 7-4.

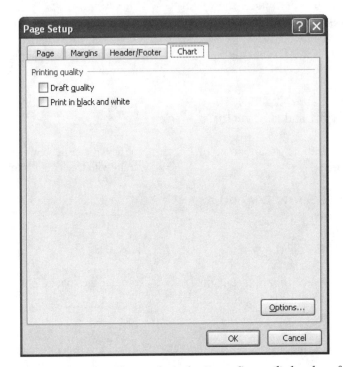

Exhibit 7-4: The Chart tab in the Page Setup dialog box for chart sheets

Do it!   **C-1:   Printing a chart**

Here's how	Here's why
1 Activate Sheet1	
Open the Print dialog box	The options available here are the same as those for worksheets.
Click **Preview**	To preview the worksheet. The footers are defined for this worksheet.
2 Click **Close Print Preview**	(In the Preview group.) To close the Print Preview window and return to the worksheet.
3 Activate the **Bonus Chart** sheet	
4 Preview the page	(Click the Office Button and choose Print, Print Preview.) The default orientation for charts is Landscape (unlike the Portrait default for worksheets). The headers and footers from the other sheet do not appear here. You can define separate headers and footers for chart sheets.
Open the Page Setup dialog box	(Click Page Setup in the Print group.) The options are the same, except that there is a Chart tab instead of a Sheet tab.
Activate the Chart tab	The dialog box resembles Exhibit 7-4.
Click **Cancel**	To close the dialog box.
5 Close the Print Preview window	
6 Update and close the workbook	

Unit summary: Creating charts

Topic A   In this topic, you learned how to create **charts** based on data in a worksheet. You learned that a chart can be created on a **chart sheet** or be **embedded** in a worksheet. You also learned how to identify various **chart objects**, such as axes, data series, data points, and the legend.

Topic B   In this topic, you learned how to modify a chart. You learned that you can select and format individual chart objects and change the **chart type**. You also learned how to move and resize an embedded chart.

Topic C   In this topic, you learned how to **print charts**. You learned that you print a chart embedded in a worksheet exactly as you print a worksheet. You also learned that the Page Setup dialog box for chart sheets contains a **Chart tab**.

Independent practice activity

In this practice activity, you'll create a column chart. You'll add a title and an axis label and modify the chart style. Then you'll format individual elements of the chart and modify the legend.

1   Open Practice chart and save it as **My practice chart**. This is a simplified projected-profits worksheet.

2   Create a two-dimensional column chart, based on the quarterly expense, revenue, and profit data. Do not include the totals data. Be sure to include the relevant text labels. (*Hint*: When inserting the chart, choose the column type **Clustered Column**.)

3   Add the chart title **Projected Profit**. (*Hint*: Activate the Layout tab.)

4   Add the value-axis label **Thousands of Dollars**.

5   Change the chart style to **Style 3**. (*Hint*: Activate the Design tab.)

6   Change the color of the Profit series to green. (*Hint*: Activate the Format tab.)

7   Move the legend below the chart. (*Hint*: Activate the Layout tab.)

8   Compare your chart to Exhibit 7-5.

9   Update and close the workbook.

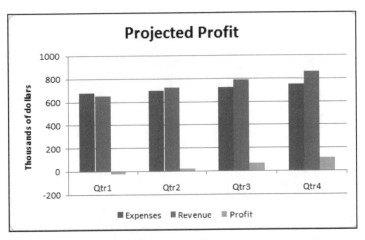

Exhibit 7-5: The worksheet after Step 8 of the independent practice activity

Review questions

1 What is a chart?

2 What is the advantage of an embedded chart?

3 List two methods of formatting chart objects.

4 List the steps you would use to add a title or axis label to a chart.

5 Can you move an embedded chart? If so, how?

Unit 8

Managing large workbooks

Unit time: 60 minutes

Complete this unit, and you'll know how to:

A Use the Freeze Panes command, split a worksheet, and hide and display both data and window elements.

B Set print titles and page breaks.

C Navigate, manage, and print multiple worksheets.

Topic A: Viewing large worksheets

This topic covers the following Microsoft Certified Applications Specialist exam objectives for Excel 2007.

#	Objective
1.4.1	Change views within a single window • Freeze and unfreeze panes • Hide the Ribbon to maximize space
1.4.2	Split windows
1.5.4	Hide and unhide worksheets
2.2.3	Hide and unhide rows and columns • Unhide a row or column • Hide a row or column

Working with large worksheets

Explanation

On a large worksheet, only part of the data is visible at one time. When you scroll through the worksheet to see the rest of the data, headings and titles move out of view, making it hard to interpret the data. You can solve this problem by using the Freeze Panes command. To make a large amount of data easier to work with, you can also hide rows, columns, and entire worksheets.

Locking row and column headings in place

The Freeze Panes command locks row or column headings in place so that headings remain visible as you scroll. To freeze rows and/or columns:

1 Select the area you want to freeze:

  • To freeze a row, select the row below it.

  • To freeze a column, select the column to its right.

  • To freeze both a row and a column, select a cell below and to the right of the row and column.

2 Activate the View tab.

3 In the Window group, click Freeze Panes and choose Freeze Panes.

To unfreeze panes, click Freeze Panes in the Window group and choose Unfreeze Panes.

Do it!

A-1: Using the Freeze Panes command

Here's how	Here's why
1 Open Large worksheet	(In the current unit folder.) You'll freeze panes to force titles and headings to remain visible when you scroll through the worksheet.
Save the workbook as **My large worksheet**	
2 Scroll the worksheet horizontally and vertically	As you scroll horizontally, the product names in column A move out of sight. When you scroll vertically, the headings in rows 4 and 5 move out of sight. To keep these names and headings in view, you can freeze the panes.
3 Select B6	To freeze row and column headings, you begin by selecting a cell below and to the right of the headings you want to freeze. By selecting B6, you'll freeze the headings in rows 1 through 5, as well as column A.
4 Activate the View tab	
In the Window group, click **Freeze Panes** and choose **Freeze Panes**	To freeze panes above and to the left of the selected cell.
5 Scroll the worksheet horizontally	To view the data in the other columns. The data in the Product column remains visible as you scroll horizontally.
6 Scroll the worksheet vertically	To view the data in the other rows. The column headings remain visible as you scroll down.
7 Click **Freeze Panes** and choose **Unfreeze Panes**	(In the Window group.) To unfreeze the rows and columns.

Splitting a worksheet

Explanation   When using large worksheets, you might need to work with sets of data in distant locations on the sheet. By splitting a worksheet into panes, you can view different areas simultaneously. When you split a window (unlike with freezing panes), you can also navigate in each pane.

You can split a worksheet horizontally, vertically, or both.

- To split a worksheet horizontally, point to the *split box* at the top of the vertical scrollbar, as shown in Exhibit 8-1. The mouse pointer changes to a *split pointer* shape, shown in Exhibit 8-2. Drag the split box down to the position where you would like to split the worksheet.

- To split a worksheet vertically, point to the split box to the right of the horizontal scrollbar, and drag to the left.

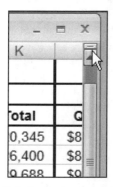

Exhibit 8-1: The split box is at the top of the scrollbar

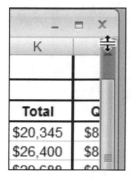

Exhibit 8-2: The split pointer

To return the split box to its original location, simply double-click it. Your worksheet will then return to a single pane.

Do it!   **A-2:   Splitting a worksheet into panes**

Here's how	Here's why
1 Point to the vertical split box	 (The vertical split box is located at the top of the vertical scrollbar.) The mouse pointer changes to a split pointer shape.
2 Drag down to row 12	To split the window into two horizontal panes. Each pane has its own scrollbar.
3 Scroll the top pane	You can navigate to any location you like.
Scroll the bottom pane	You can navigate independently from the top pane.
4 In the top pane, edit the value of B6 to be **$6,500**	Select the cell and type 6500.
5 In the bottom pane, scroll until B6 is visible	The value of B6 has changed to $6,500 in the lower pane. Excel keeps the two panes in sync.
6 Double-click the bar that separates the two panes	To return the worksheet to a single pane.
7 Point to the horizontal split box	 (The horizontal split box is located on the right side of the horizontal scrollbar, near the bottom of the Excel window.) The mouse pointer changes to a split pointer shape.
Drag left to column F	To split the worksheet into two vertical panes.
Scroll the left and right panes	To navigate in each pane.
Double-click the bar that separates the two panes	To return the worksheet to a single pane.
8 Update the workbook	

The Hide and Unhide commands

Explanation   Individual rows and columns can be hidden from view. This is useful when you want to focus on specific data, or when you want to conceal formulas or other information.

To hide a column:

1   Select a column or a range of columns to be hidden.
2   Activate the Home tab.
3   In the Cells group, click Format and choose Hide & Unhide, Hide Columns.

You can also hide columns by selecting them, right-clicking, and choosing Hide.

Exhibit 8-3 displays a worksheet showing only the Total columns F, K, P, U, and Z. The columns in between—the columns containing quarterly sales details—are hidden.

You'll unhide rows and columns when you want to use or view them again. To unhide columns:

1   Select the columns on either side of the hidden column or range of columns.
2   Activate the Home tab.
3   In the Cells group, click Format and choose Hide & Unhide, Unhide Columns.

Similarly, you can hide and unhide entire worksheets.

1   Select a worksheet tab.
2   Activate the Home tab.
3   In the Cells group, click Format and choose Hide & Unhide, Hide Sheet.

You can also hide worksheets by right-clicking the sheet tab and choosing Hide. Unhide a worksheet as you would a row or column.

	A	F	K	P	U	Z
1	**Outlander Spices**					
2	**Bonus sales for all regions**					
3						
4		**North**	**South**	**East**	**Central**	**West**
5	**Product**	**Total**	**Total**	**Total**	**Total**	**Total**
6	Dill Seed	$23,442	$20,345	$29,196	$35,902	$23,442
7	Mustard Seed	$24,755	$26,400	$34,879	$41,886	$24,755
8	Coriander Powder	$23,765	$29,688	$28,689	$36,485	$23,765
9	Turmeric	$23,831	$23,055	$37,545	$36,461	$23,831
10	Cinnamon (Ground Korintje)	$26,466	$33,404	$19,761	$41,993	$26,466
11	Cinnamon (Ground) Xtra Hi Oil (2x)	$1,845	$2,253	$2,139	$2,644	$1,845
12	Cinnamon (Ground) High Oil (1X)	$1,753	$2,146	$1,871	$2,819	$1,753

Exhibit 8-3: A sales worksheet with regional sales columns hidden

Do it!   **A-3:   Hiding and unhiding columns and worksheets**

Here's how	Here's why
1 Select columns B:E	You'll hide detail columns so that only the totals appear.
2 Activate the Home tab	If necessary
In the Cells group, click **Format** and choose **Hide & Unhide**, **Hide Columns**	To hide the quarterly sales details and display only the total sales for the North region.
3 Select columns G:J	You'll hide these columns by using another method.
Right-click the selection and choose **Hide**	To hide the quarterly sales details and display only the total sales for the South region.
4 Hide the quarterly sales details for the remaining regions	(Select the columns you want to hide, right-click a selected column's heading, and choose Hide.) To display only the total sales columns for the five regions, as shown in Exhibit 8-3.
5 Select columns A:Z	You'll unhide the columns. To unhide columns B:Y, you must select the columns surrounding them.
6 Right-click and choose **Unhide**	To unhide columns B:Y. The worksheet now displays the quarterly sales details for the regions again.
7 Activate the Product details worksheet	
8 Right-click the **Product details** sheet tab and choose **Hide**	The view returns to the Regional sales sheet. The tab for the Product details sheet is no longer visible.
9 Right-click the **Regional sales** sheet tab and choose **Unhide...**	To open the Unhide dialog box. The Product details sheet is selected. It is the only sheet currently hidden in this workbook.
Click **OK**	To close the dialog box, unhide the Product details sheet, and activate that sheet.
Return to the Regional sales sheet	

Minimize the Ribbon to view more data

Explanation

You can minimize the Ribbon in order to view more of the worksheet data. When you minimize the Ribbon, the tabs are still visible. You can use the options on each tab by clicking the tab to make them visible. When you're done using the tab options, the Ribbon is minimized again.

To minimize the Ribbon, click the Customize Quick Access Toolbar button on the Quick Access toolbar, and choose Minimize the Ribbon. Choose it again to maximize the Ribbon.

Do it!

A-4:   Minimizing the Ribbon

Here's how	Here's why
1 Click as shown	
	To display the Customize Quick Access Toolbar menu.
2 Choose **Minimize the Ribbon**	To minimize the Ribbon. The tabs are still visible.
3 Select B5:F5	
Activate the Home tab	The Home tab options appear. You'll apply formatting to the range.
Apply the italic style to the selected range	After the option is applied, the Home tab options are hidden again.
4 Undo the formatting	Click the Undo button.
5 Maximize the Ribbon	Display the Customize Quick Access Toolbar menu and uncheck Minimize the Ribbon.
6 Update the workbook	

Topic B: Printing large worksheets

This topic covers the following Microsoft Certified Applications Specialist exam objectives for Excel 2007.

#	Objective
1.4.1	**Change views within a single window**
	• Page break preview
5.5.2	**Insert and move a page break**
	• Preview and change a page break from the third to the fourth column

Preparing to print

Explanation

Before you print large worksheets, you'll probably want to set print titles and specify where page breaks should appear.

Print titles

Before printing a large worksheet, preview it to see how it will appear when printed. You'll notice that your data headings appear on only the first page. This makes the data on the other pages hard to interpret. You can set *print titles* to specify which text should print as headings on all pages.

To set print titles for a worksheet:

1 Activate the Page Layout tab.

2 In the Page Setup group, click Print Titles. The Page Setup dialog box opens with the Sheet tab active.

3 Under Print titles, enter the range containing the titles that you want to print on each page. You can select the rows to repeat at the top of all pages, columns to repeat on the left side of all pages, or both.

4 Click OK.

Do it!

B-1: Setting print titles

Here's how	Here's why
1 Preview the worksheet	(Click the Office Button and choose Print, Print Preview.) You'll preview the Regional sales worksheet to see how it will look when printed.
View the whole page	If necessary, click the page or the Zoom button to zoom out.
2 In the Print Preview group, click **Next Page** twice	To move to the third page of data in the preview. The data on this page doesn't have row titles and is difficult to interpret. You'll add print titles to all the pages.
3 In the Preview group, click **Close Print Preview**	To close the preview window and return to the worksheet.
4 Activate the Page Layout tab	If necessary.
5 In the Page Setup group, click **Print Titles**	To open the Page Setup dialog box. The Sheet tab is active by default.
Under Print titles, in the "Rows to repeat at top" box, click 📇	(The Collapse Dialog button.) The "Page Setup - Rows to repeat at top" dialog box appears.
Select rows 1 through 5	

	A
1	**Outlander Spices**
2	**Bonus sales for all regions**
3	
4	
➡5	**Product**

	To designate these rows as print titles. A dashed line surrounds the selected rows.
6 Click 🔲	(The Collapse Dialog button is in the "Page Setup - Rows to repeat at top" dialog box.) To return to the Page Setup dialog box.
7 Select column A as the print title	To print the entire column on the left side of each page. (Click the Collapse Dialog button beside "Columns to repeat at left." Then select column A, and click the Collapse Dialog button to return to the Page Setup dialog box.)
Click **OK**	To close the Page Setup dialog box.
8 Preview the worksheet	

9 Press `PAGE DOWN` twice

To see the third page. The regional titles above the quarters columns change, but the top and left titles remain the same.

View the other pages

Close the preview

10 Update the workbook

Page breaks

Explanation

Excel inserts automatic page breaks that determine how worksheet data will be divided among the printed pages. Sometimes, sets of information that should appear together will fall on separate pages. To change this, you can insert manual page breaks, which appear as solid lines in the worksheet window, or preview the automatic page breaks and adjust them.

To insert a vertical page break, select the column to the left of where you want to place the page break. (To insert a horizontal page break, select the row above where you want to insert the page break.) Activate the Page Layout tab. In the Page Setup group, click Breaks and choose Insert Page Break.

Page Break Preview

Page Break Preview shows you where page breaks will occur when a worksheet is printed. You can drag page breaks to new positions if necessary.

To preview page breaks, click the Page Break Preview button on the right side of the status bar. Manually inserted page breaks appear as solid blue lines. Automatically inserted page breaks appear as dashed blue lines, as shown in Exhibit 8-4.

	A	B	C	D	E	F	G	H	I	J	K	L	M
1	**Outlander Spices**												
2	Bonus sales for all regions												
3													
4				North			South						
5	**Product**	**Qtr1**	**Qtr2**	**Qtr3**	**Qtr4**	**Total**	**Qtr1**	**Qtr2**	**Qtr3**	**Qtr4**	**Total**	**Qtr1**	**Qtr2**
6	Dill Seed	$6,354	$4,846	$3,958	$8,284	$23,442	$5,235	$6,333	$2,535	$6,242	$20,345	$8,990	$9,452
7	Mustard Seed	$8,484	$5,858	$5,858	$4,555	$24,755	$3,041	$8,364	$6,349	$2,646	$26,400	$8,926	$8,922
8	Coriander Powder	$9,595	$5,859	$4,879	$3,432	$23,765	$10,243	$8,925	$5,254	$5,266	$29,688	$9,827	$6,782
9	Turmeric	$7,578	$6,900	$3,444	$5,909	$23,831	$8,457	$2,466	$7,466	$4,666	$23,055	$8,922	$9,892
10	Cinnamon (Ground Korintje)	$6,291	$5,209	$6,333	$8,633	$26,466	$9,457	$7,457	$7,545	$8,945	$33,404	$2,266	$7,225
11	Cinnamon (Ground) Xtra Hi Oil (2	$791	$278	$298	$478	$1,845	$734	$642	$345	$532	$2,253	$634	$643
12	Cinnamon (Ground) High Oil (1X)	$432	$322	$245	$754	$1,753	$436	$733	$634	$343	$2,146	$343	$633
13	Angelica Root	$6,354	$6,563	$4,333	$8,284	$25,534	$3,466	$2,662	$6,422	$6,222	$18,772	$4,632	$7,222
14	Anise	$789	$434	$564	$633	$2,420	$422	$624	$733	$732	$2,511	$574	$553
15	Anise Seeds	$534	$423	$521	$625	$2,103	$833	$733	$1,065	$1,198	$3,829	$734	$457
16	Annatto Seed	$644	$643	$634	$632	$2,553	$636	$732	$477	$845	$2,690	$856	$856
17	Asafoetida Powder	$654	$634	$326	$754	$2,368	$753	$844	$1,024	$1,157	$3,778	$688	$468
18	Basil Leaf (Whole)	$6,778	$6,760	$4,568	$7,834	$25,940	$8,566	$9,556	$8,554	$7,886	$34,562	$9,555	$5,975
19	Basil Leaf (Ground)	$6,354	$6,346	$3,555	$6,442	$22,697	$7,464	$8,444	$5,858	$8,445	$30,211	$7,866	$9,559
20	Bay Leaf (Whole)	$233	$532	$525	$652	$1,942	$577	$855	$844	$734	$3,010	$667	$799
21	Bay Leaf (Ground)	$543	$634	$744	$543	$2,464	$733	$742	$983	$732	$3,190	$595	$599
22	Caraway Seed (Whole)	$354	$633	$422	$255	$1,664	$854	$966	$673	$755	$3,248	$676	$856
23	Caraway Seed (Ground)	$532	$526	$355	$644	$2,057	$735	$834	$375	$357	$2,301	$686	$486
24	Cardamom Seed (Whole)	$255	$525	$252	$624	$1,656	$357	$733	$753	$632	$2,475	$379	$375
25	Cardamom Seed (Ground)	$422	$642	$642	$624	$2,330	$822	$583	$833	$834	$3,072	$844	$848

Exhibit 8-4: Page Break Preview, showing automatic and manual page breaks

Do it!

B-2:   Adjusting page breaks

Here's how	Here's why
1 Click [⊞]	(The Page Break Preview button is on the right side of the status bar.) You'll view the page breaks for this worksheet and set manual page breaks by dragging the page breaks to new locations.
Observe the screen	A solid blue line between columns C and D indicates a manual page break.
2 Point as shown	
	The pointer changes to a double-headed arrow, indicating that the page break can be moved.
Drag the page break to between columns D and E	This is still an incorrect placement, as it splits the North region's sales data unnecessarily.
3 Activate the Page Layout tab	If necessary.
Select column E	
In the Page Setup group, click **Breaks**	To display a menu.
Choose **Remove Page Break**	To delete the manual page break.
4 Deselect the column	
Observe the screen	Dashed blue lines, indicating automatic page breaks, appear on the worksheet. Page numbers appear in the background. You'll set a manual page break after each year's Total column by dragging the automatic page breaks. The first automatic page break is visible after the Qtr1 column in the South region.

5	Point to the first automatic-page-break line	(The page-break line is between columns G and H.) The pointer changes to a double-headed arrow.
	Drag the pointer to the right edge of column F	To move the page-break line, inserting a manual page break after column F. The page-break line is now a solid blue line between columns F and G. Now, only data for the North region appears on the first page.
	Observe the next page break	The automatic page break that was between columns M and N has moved to the left. This occurred because when you move one page break, the other automatic page breaks move automatically. You'll move the other page breaks so that each region appears on a separate page.
6	Move the second page break to enclose only the South region	Point to the page-break line between columns L and M. The pointer changes to a double-headed arrow. Drag the page break to the left until it is between columns K and L.
	Place a page break after each remaining region	Drag each to the left.
7	Scroll down to row 57	Another user inserted a manual page break at row 57, which forces unneeded pages to be created. You'll move this page break.
	Move the page break to just after the Totals row	Drag the solid blue bar up to between rows 41 and 42.
8	Preview the worksheet	All of the data for the North region appears by itself on the first page.
	Preview the other pages	(In the Print Preview group, click Next Page.) Each region's data appears on its own page.
	Close Print Preview	In the Preview group, click Close Print Preview.
9	Update and close the workbook	

Topic C: Using multiple worksheets

This topic covers the following Microsoft Certified Applications Specialist exam objectives for Excel 2007.

#	Objective
1.5.1	Copy worksheets
	• Within a workbook
1.5.2	Reposition worksheets within workbooks
1.5.3	Rename worksheets
1.5.5	Insert and delete worksheets
2.1.3	Add color to worksheet tabs

Options for working with multiple worksheets

Explanation

An Excel workbook can contain multiple worksheets that store related information conveniently in a single file. You can move easily among the worksheets. You can also rename worksheets, change the color of the sheet tabs, insert, move, copy, and delete sheets, and print multiple sheets.

Navigating among worksheets

Tabs at the bottom of the window provide access to each sheet, as shown in Exhibit 8-5. Press Ctrl+Page Down to move to the next sheet in a workbook, and press Ctrl+Page Up to move to the previous sheet.

If your workbook contains more than a few worksheets, Excel might not be able to display all the sheet tabs at the same time. Click the tab scrolling buttons to reveal the hidden tabs.

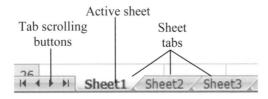

Exhibit 8-5: The tab scrolling buttons and sheet tabs

Do it!

C-1: Navigating between worksheets

Here's how	Here's why
1 Open Navigate	(In the current unit folder.) The Navigate workbook consists of eight worksheets. Sheet1 is active and contains the bonus sales report for the North region for 2006. You'll use the sheet tabs to switch between worksheets.
Save the workbook as **My navigate**	In the current unit folder.
2 Click the **Sheet2** tab	To view the data in the Sheet2 worksheet. It contains the 2006 bonus sales report for the South region.
3 Activate Sheet3	(Click the Sheet3 tab.) To view the 2005 bonus sales report for the North region.
4 Activate the Bonus Sales Report sheet	This worksheet contains the bonus sales report for the North and South regions for the years 2004–2006.
5 Click as shown	 (The tab scrolling buttons are to the left of the sheet tabs.) To fully display the Consolidate sheet tab. The Sheet1 tab is no longer visible.
6 Click [◄]	To display the Sheet1 tab.

Renaming worksheets

Explanation

By default, Excel names new worksheets consecutively as Sheet1, Sheet2, Sheet3, and so forth, but you can give worksheets more meaningful names. There are three ways to rename a worksheet:

- Double-click the sheet tab.
- Right-click the sheet tab and choose Rename.
- Activate the Home tab. In the Cells group, click Format and choose Rename Sheet.

Any of these methods selects the name in the sheet tab. Type the new name and press Enter.

Formatting worksheet tabs

You can also color-code worksheet tabs so that it's easier to identify related sheets at a glance, as shown in Exhibit 8-6. Here's how:

1 Right-click the worksheet tab to display a shortcut menu.
2 Choose Tab Color to open the Theme Colors box.
3 Select the color you want to apply.

| North 2006 | South 2006 | North 2005 | South 2005 | North 2004 | South 2004 |

Exhibit 8-6: Sheet tabs can be color-coded

Do it!

C-2: Naming worksheets and coloring tabs

Here's how	Here's why
1 Double-click **Sheet1**	To select the text "Sheet1."
Type **North 2006**	
Press (↵ ENTER)	To change the name of the sheet to "North 2006." This name better identifies the sheet's contents.
2 Right-click **Sheet2**	To display a shortcut menu.
Choose **Rename**	
Type **South 2006**	
Press (↵ ENTER)	
3 Rename Sheet3 and Sheet4 as **North 2005** and **South 2005**, respectively	Double-click the sheet tab, enter the name, and press Enter.
4 Rename Sheet5 and Sheet6 as **North 2004** and **South 2004**, respectively	
5 Right-click **North 2006**	You might need to click a tab scrolling button to display the sheet tab.
Choose **Tab Color**	To display the Colors gallery. You'll color-code tabs to clearly identify related sheets.
Select the indicated color	

	To make this tab green.
Activate the South 2006 sheet	The color of the North 2006 tab changes to green.
6 Apply the green color to the North 2005 and North 2004 tabs	(Right-click the sheet tab and choose Tab Color.) To color both worksheet tabs green.

7 Change the color of the three South tabs to blue

(Select any shade of blue from the Colors gallery.) The color coding helps you distinguish between the South and North region sheets. The tabs should resemble those in Exhibit 8-6.

8 Update and close the workbook

Managing multiple worksheets

Explanation

You can insert, move, copy, and delete worksheets within a workbook, just as you can insert, move, copy, or delete other items.

Inserting worksheets

When you insert a worksheet, Excel places it before the active worksheet. You can insert a new worksheet by using any of the following techniques:

- Activate the Home tab. In the Cells group, click the Insert button's down-arrow and choose Insert Sheet.
- Right-click a worksheet tab and choose Insert. Select Worksheet from the Insert dialog box and click OK.
- Press Shift+F11.

Moving and copying worksheets

You can move or copy worksheets within a workbook, or to another workbook, by using the Move or Copy dialog box. You can also move a worksheet by dragging it to a new location. To copy a worksheet, press Ctrl and drag the sheet to a new location.

To use the Move or Copy dialog box:

1. Activate the Home tab.
2. In the Cells group, click Format and choose Move or Copy Sheet to open the Move or Copy dialog box.
3. Select a new location for the worksheet from either the To book list or the Before sheet list.
4. If you want to copy the sheet (rather than move it), check Create a copy.
5. Click OK.

Deleting worksheets

When you're deleting a worksheet that contains data, Excel prompts you to confirm the deletion because you cannot undo this action.

To delete multiple worksheets at the same time, you need to select them. To do so, click the first sheet tab, press Ctrl, and click the other sheet tabs. Then do either of the following:

- Activate the Home tab. In the Cells group, click Delete and choose Delete Sheet.
- Right-click the sheet tab and choose Delete.

Do it!

C-3: Working with multiple worksheets

Here's how	Here's why
1 Open Yearly sales	The Yearly sales workbook consists of seven worksheets. The North, South, East, and West worksheets contain regional sales reports. The other worksheets summarize data from the individual regions.
Save the workbook as **My yearly sales**	In the current unit folder.
2 Activate the Report sheet	This worksheet contains the total sales for all regions. You'll insert a new worksheet, named Sheet1, before the Report worksheet.
3 Activate the Home tab	If necessary.
In the Cells group, click as shown	
Choose **Insert Sheet**	To insert a new worksheet, named Sheet1, before the Report worksheet.
4 Right-click the **Report** sheet tab and choose **Insert...**	To open the Insert dialog box. The General tab is activated, and Worksheet is selected by default.
Click **OK**	To insert a new worksheet, named Sheet2, before the Report sheet.
5 Rename Sheet1 as **International**	
6 In the Cells group, click **Format** and choose **Move or Copy Sheet...**	To open the Move or Copy dialog box.
From the Before sheet list, select **Consolidating data**	
Click **OK**	To move the International worksheet before the Consolidating data worksheet.
7 Activate the International sheet	(If necessary.) You'll move the worksheet again.
Drag the sheet tab to the left of the Report tab	To move the International worksheet.

8	Right-click the **Sheet2** tab	This sheet is not needed.
	Choose **Delete**	To remove Sheet2 from the workbook.
9	Activate the Report sheet	You'll copy this sheet.
	In the Cells group, click **Format** and choose **Move or Copy Sheet...**	To open the Move or Copy dialog box.
	Check **Create a copy**	
	Click **OK**	Excel copies the sheet with the name Report (2) and places it before the first sheet in the workbook.
10	Activate the original Report sheet	You'll delete this sheet.
	In the Cells group, click **Delete** and choose **Delete Sheet**	A message box appears, warning that the sheet contains data.
	Click **Delete**	To permanently delete the Report sheet.
	Rename the Report (2) worksheet as **Report**	
11	Update the workbook	

Printing multiple worksheets

Explanation

You can print multiple worksheets at the same time. To do so, select the worksheets that you want to print, and then open the Print dialog box. To select multiple worksheets, press and hold Ctrl, and click the worksheet tabs. Multiple worksheets can also be displayed in Print Preview.

Do it!

C-4:   Previewing and printing multiple worksheets

Here's how	Here's why
1 Activate the North sheet	You might need to click a tab scrolling button to display this sheet.
Press ⟨CTRL⟩ and click the **South**, **East**, and **West** tabs	To add the South, East, and West sheets to the selection.
Release ⟨CTRL⟩	
2 Preview the worksheet in Print Preview	You'll see that the four worksheets are ready to print, each on a separate page.
In the Print Preview group, click **Next Page**	To preview the South sheet.
Preview the East sheet	Click Next Page.
Click **Previous Page**	To go back to the South sheet.
3 Return to the North sheet	
In the Preview group, click **Close Print Preview**	To close the preview.
4 Click	
Choose **Print**, **Quick Print**	To print all four worksheets with the current print settings.
5 Update and close the workbook	

Unit summary: Managing large workbooks

Topic A   In this topic, you learned how to **freeze panes** to keep selected row or column headings and groups of cells in place as you scroll through a worksheet. Then, you learned how to **split panes** to access two worksheet sections simultaneously. Finally, you learned how to **hide** and **unhide** columns, rows, and worksheets to display only the data you need.

Topic B   In this topic, you learned how to set **print titles** so that headings appear on every page. Next, you learned how to set **page breaks**. Finally, you used the **Page Break Preview** feature to view and adjust page breaks.

Topic C   In this topic, you learned how to navigate between **multiple worksheets** and how to improve worksheet identification by renaming worksheets and adding color to their tabs. You also learned how to insert, copy, move, and delete worksheets and how to preview and print multiple worksheets.

Independent practice activity

In this activity, you will freeze panes, hide and unhide data, and set print titles. Then you'll use Page Break Preview to set page breaks. Finally, you'll insert, rename, and move worksheets.

1 Open Practice sales data (from the current unit folder), and save it as **My practice sales data**.

2 Freeze the information in column A and rows 1-4. Scroll vertically and horizontally, and then unfreeze the information.

3 Hide these columns: Units purchased, Cost per unit, Units sold, Selling price per unit, and Units on hand.

4 Unhide all the hidden columns.

5 If necessary, scroll vertically and horizontally to view all of the rows and columns.

6 Minimize, and then maximize, the Ribbon.

7 Set print titles so that the company name, subtitle, product names, and region names appear on every page. (*Hint:* Make the first four rows and the first two columns appear on every printed page.)

8 Use Page Break Preview to adjust the page breaks so that data appears on two pages.

9 Preview the worksheet, zoom in, and compare the preview of the second page with Exhibit 8-7.

10 Rename Sheet2 to **Totals**.

11 Color the Totals sheet tab red.

12 Insert a new worksheet, name it **International**, and move it to the right of Totals.

13 Update and close the workbook.

14 Close Excel.

Outlander Spices
Purchase/sales report

Product	Region	Selling price per unit	Total sale	Units on hand	Total value of stock
Cinnamon (Ground Korintje)	East	$50	$80,000	32	$640
Cinnamon (Ground) Extra High Oil (2X)	East	$35	$57,750	80	$1,760
Cinnamon (Ground) High Oil (1X)	East	$40	$44,000	139	$4,726
Angelica Root	East	$65	$97,500	209	$7,106
Anise	East	$60	$80,700	84	$3,780
Anise Seeds	East	$70	$91,770	188	$9,964
Annatto Speed	East	$50	$89,450	195	$4,485
Asafoetida Powder	East	$33	$22,770	356	$4,628
Sub Total(East)			$563,940	1,283	$37,089
Basil Leaf (Whole)	North	$125	$250,000	1,904	$156,128
Basil Leaf (Ground)	North	$96	$48,000	1,494	$62,748
Bay Leaf (Whole)	North	$35	$245,000	1,984	$23,808
Bay Leaf (Ground)	North	$45	$292,500	3,500	$122,500
Caraway Seed (Whole)	North	$25	$28,475	620	$10,540
Caraway Seed (Ground)	North	$30	$160,230	2,142	$57,834
Cardamom Seed (Whole)	North	$30	$228,360	6,729	$174,954
Cardamom Seed (Ground)	North	$25	$168,075	2,060	$39,140
Carob Powder (Raw)	North	$27	$213,921	1,388	$31,924
Carob Pods (Ribbled)	North	$35	$31,500	960	$30,720

Exhibit 8-7: A sample preview of the second page after Step 8 of the independent practice activity

Review questions

1 When you're working with a large worksheet, how can you lock row or column headings in place so that when you scroll, these headings will remain visible?

2 What is the difference between freezing panes and splitting windows?

3 A worksheet can be split either horizontally or vertically, but not both simultaneously. True or false?

4 You can insert both vertical and horizontal page breaks in a worksheet. True or false?

5 List three methods you can use to change a worksheet name.

Course summary

This summary contains information to help you bring the course to a successful conclusion. Using this information, you will be able to:

A Use the summary text to reinforce what you've learned in class.

B Determine the next courses in this series (if any), as well as any other resources that might help you continue to learn about Excel 2007.

Topic A: Course summary

Use the following summary text to reinforce what you've learned in class.

Unit summaries

Unit 1

In this unit, you learned how to start Microsoft Excel and identify the main components of the **Excel window**. You learned that Excel files are called **workbooks**, which consist of **worksheets** that are arranged in rows and columns. Then, you learned how to use the Help feature. Finally, you learned how to open and **navigate** a workbook.

Unit 2

In this unit, you learned how to enter and edit **text**, **values**, and **formulas** and how to insert, move, and resize **pictures**. In addition, you learned how to **autofill** cells. Finally, you learned how to **save** and update a workbook, and use the Compatibility Checker.

Unit 3

In this unit, you learned how to move and copy data by using the **Cut**, **Copy**, and **Paste** commands. You also learned how to copy data by using the **drag-and-drop** method and by using the Windows and Office **Clipboards**. Next, you learned how to move and copy formulas. Then, you learned the difference between **relative** and **absolute references** and why both are necessary. Finally, you learned how to insert and delete ranges and entire rows and columns.

Unit 4

In this unit, you learned that **functions** are predefined formulas that perform specific calculations. You learned that a function can include **arguments** on which to perform its calculations, and that Excel can **trace errors** and correct simple syntax errors. You also learned how to use the **SUM** function, as well as how to use the **AutoSum** feature to enter SUM functions quickly in a cell or range. Finally, you learned how to use the **AVERAGE**, **MIN**, **MAX**, **COUNT**, and **COUNTA** functions.

Unit 5

In this unit, you learned how to apply **text formatting**. Next, you learned how to change the **column width** and **row height** and how to control alignment of data within a cell. In addition, you learned how to **format numbers** as currency or percentages and how to adjust the number of decimal places in a number. Next, you learned how to apply **conditional formats**. Finally, you learned how to copy formats and use table formats.

Unit 6

In this unit, you learned how to use the **spelling checker** to proof your work and use the Research task pane to find word definitions and synonyms. You used the **Print Preview** command to see how a printed worksheet will look before printing. Next, you learned how to use **Page Setup** to control the appearance of printouts. You learned how to set margins, display gridlines, and create custom headers and footers. Finally, you learned how to set and clear a **print area** and how to use the **Print dialog box** to print a worksheet.

Unit 7

In this unit, you learned the basics of creating and formatting **charts**. You learned how to change the **chart type** and format chart elements. You also learned how to move and resize embedded charts. Finally, you learned how to print charts.

Unit 8

In this unit, you learned how to navigate between worksheets. Next, you learned how to rename and **color-code** worksheet tabs. Then you learned how to insert, copy, move, and delete worksheets. Finally, you learned how to preview and print multiple worksheets.

Topic B: Continued learning after class

It is impossible to learn to use any software effectively in a single day. To get the most out of this class, you should begin working with Microsoft Excel 2007 to perform real tasks as soon as possible. We also offer resources for continued learning.

Next courses in this series

This is the first course in this series. The next courses in this series are:

- *Excel 2007: Intermediate*
  - Link worksheets and workbooks
  - Create outlines and consolidate data
  - Use subtotals in worksheets
  - Sort and filter data
  - Create tables
  - Publish worksheets to the Web
  - Use advanced formatting techniques
  - Create complex charts
- *Excel 2007: Advanced*
  - Use advanced formulas and functions
  - Set up data validation
  - Create PivotTables and PivotCharts
  - Import and export data
  - Use data analysis tools
  - Create and run macros
  - Use database functions
  - Create custom functions
- *Excel 2007: Power User*
  - Create 3-D charts
  - Use complex functions
  - Use graphics effectively
  - Set advanced customization options
  - Embed and link objects in worksheets
  - Use statistical analysis tools and wizards
  - Work with custom Smart Tags
  - Apply advanced formatting commands

- *Excel 2007: VBA Programming*
  - Use the Visual Basic Editor
  - Work with object properties and methods
  - Attach code to buttons
  - Use variables, expressions, and procedures
  - Create decision and loop structures
  - Add user forms to worksheets
  - Identify coding errors
  - Use debugging tools

Other resources

For more information, visit www.axzopress.com.

Excel 2007: Basic

Quick reference

Button	Shortcut keys	Function
⑦	F1	Opens the Microsoft Excel Help window.
Picture		Inserts a picture from a file.
▣	ALT + 5	Creates a new folder.
↶	CTRL + Z	Undoes the last action.
💾	CTRL + S	Saves the current workbook in its current folder.
✂	CTRL + X	Cuts the selected data to the Clipboard.
📋	CTRL + V	Pastes data from the Clipboard to the selected location.
📑	CTRL + C	Copies the selected data to the Clipboard.
f_x	SHIFT + F3	Opens the Insert Function dialog box.
Σ	ALT + =	Inserts an AutoSum function.
B	CTRL + B	Applies bold formatting to the selection.
I	CTRL + I	Applies italics to the selection.
≡		Centers the selection.
≡		Right-aligns the selection.

Button	Function
	Merges and centers the selection.
	Applies a border to the bottom of the selected range.
	Decreases the number of decimal places.
	Launches a dialog box from a Ribbon group.
	Copies the format of the selected cell or range.
	In the Table Styles group, displays the list of table styles.
	Changes the worksheet display to Page Layout view.
	Changes the worksheet display to Normal view.
	Collapses a dialog box.
	Expands a dialog box.
	Sorts a list in ascending order.
	Changes the worksheet to display Page Break Preview.

Glossary

Absolute reference
When copying a formula, this type of cell or range address remains unchanged.

Alignment
Refers to the placement of data within a cell.

Argument
The input value of a function.

AutoFormat
A predefined combination of text formatting, number formatting, borders, colors, and shading that you can apply in a single step.

AutoSum button
Automatically generates a SUM function for you.

Cell
The intersection of a row and a column in a worksheet, used to contain various kinds of data that you can format, sort, and analyze.

Chart
A pictorial representation of worksheet data.

Clear
A command that you can use to remove a cell's contents, formats, comments, or all three.

Clipboard
A temporary storage area that holds the specified data until you identify where to place it in a worksheet.

Column
A vertical group of cells in a worksheet.

Dragging
Refers to the action of pointing to a cell, pressing the mouse button, and moving the pointer without releasing the mouse button.

Dropping
Refers to the action of releasing the mouse button after the pointer reaches the destination cell.

Embedded chart
A pictorial representation of worksheet data that is placed as an object in a worksheet.

Error indicator
A green triangle located in the top-left corner of a cell containing an incorrect formula.

Function
A predefined formula that performs calculations, which can range from simple to complex.

Hyperlink
Text or a graphic that, when clicked, takes you to another place in the same document or to another document entirely.

Label
Text that identifies the data entered in a worksheet.

Mixed reference
A cell or range address that has either an absolute column and relative row, or absolute row and relative column.

Non-contiguous range
A selected group of cells located in different (non-adjacent) areas of the worksheet.

Operator
A symbol included in a formula to indicate the type of calculation to be performed, such as multiplication, subtraction, etc.

Print area
One or more ranges of cells that you designate to be printed.

Range
A selection that includes multiple consecutive cells.

Reference
Identifies a cell or a range of cells in a worksheet.

Relative cell reference
When a copying a formula, this type of cell or range address is updated in relation to the location of the formula.

Row
A horizontal group of cells in a worksheet.

Shortcut menu
Provides a short list of commands related to the object or screen element to which you're pointing.

Template
A special workbook that contains formatting, data, and tools to help you create specific types of workbooks, such as invoices and expense reports.

URL (Uniform Resource Locator)

An address for a file on the Internet.

Value

The raw data in a worksheet.

Weibull distribution

A complex calculation used in reliability analysis, such as to calculate a device's mean time to failure.

Workbook

An Excel file which contains multiple worksheets.

Worksheet

A document that consists of intersecting rows and columns which contain data.

Index